The Rise and Fall of Putinism, and the Stakes of a Global War

Cherry
Orchard
Books

THE RISE AND FALL OF PUTINISM, AND THE STAKES OF A GLOBAL WAR

Andrei Piontkovsky

Translated and Edited by
Jason Galie

BOSTON
2026

Library of Congress Cataloging-in-Publication Data:
Print LCCN
2025035395

ISBN 9798887198354 (Hardback)
ISBN 9798887198361 (Paperback)
ISBN 9798887198378 (Adobe PDF)
ISBN 9798887198385 (ePub)

Book design by Kryon Publishing & Data
https://www.kryonpublishing.com/
Cover artwork by Eiko Ojala © 2026

*The author would like to express his gratitude to
Leonid Nevzlin and the Renewing Democracy Initiative
for their generous support of this publication.*

Contents

Preface

A Prophet in an Alien Land
Leonid Nevzlin

What goes through the mind of a man who has issued warning after warning about an imminent catastrophe and then watches as each and every one of his predictions comes true? What should he do when the catastrophe comes to pass?

These were the thoughts foremost in my mind as I revisited Andrei Andreyevich Piontkovsky's collected works, written over the course of almost a quarter century. These writings dissect a nation's gradual shift from a so-called "New Russia" to an aggressive, fascist state capable of unleashing a terrible war against Ukraine and threatening the entire world with nuclear apocalypse. We all bore witness to the profound moral decline and dehumanization of society in the parts of the world which Piontkovsky refers to as Putinstan.

From the moment Putin arrived on the political scene, Andrei Andreyevich saw the makings of a totalitarian regime taking hold in Russia. Even in this early period, the so-called "days of a beautiful dawning," when Putin was regarded both within Russia and abroad as, to use the satirist Saltykov-Shchedrin's expression, "the cat's meow," Piontkovsky did not fall for the ostensible charms of this KGB lieutenant colonel. He did not join the chorus of Joseph Brodsky aficionados who were quick to quote a line from his "Letter to the Roman Friend": "I prefer a robber to a butcher." He was well aware that a robber can also be a butcher, or even a murderer.

In January 2000, Piontkovsky published an article entitled "Putinism as the Highest and Final Stage of Bandit Capitalism in Russia." The text outlined the final stages of a process that saw Russia move from an autocratic regime to a mafia-based one. This mafia regime was prepared, for the sake of "consolidating the nation" and, essentially, retaining power, to unleash a war against a one-time "fraternal people." In so doing, it made widespread use of the most despicable, chauvinistic slogans. Piontkovsky referred to Putinism as the "control shot" to the head of Russia and compared Yeltsin, who named Putin as his successor, to Hindenburg, the man who appointed Hitler as Reich Chancellor.

Piontkovsky has always called a spade a spade, unafraid to speak openly about things most people only whispered about. To me, this brand of courage, this categorical refusal to conform is the most crucial attribute of a true member of the intelligentsia.

Indeed, Andrei Andreyevich is a third-generation member of this intelligentsia. The fate of his family was as tragic as it was typical for members of this group under Stalin. Piontkovsky's father and grandfather were prominent legal scholars. An uncle, Sergei Andreyevich Piontkovsky, was a historian executed in 1937. One could say that Andrei Andreyevich has an almost biological respect for law and justice and an equally strong abhorrence of the gangster "code of conduct."

Andrei Andreyevich was raised in a family with strong humanist traditions. And yet, he chose a different path for himself—the Mechanics and Mathematics Department at Moscow State University. Piontkovsky is a serious scholar, the author of over 100 articles and several monographs: on control theory, global modeling, and nuclear strategy. For many years he worked at the Institute for Systems Analysis at the Soviet (then Russian) Academy of Sciences. It must be mentioned that this was an extremely atypical Soviet institution, affiliated with the International Institute for Applied Systems Analysis (IIASA) headquartered in Austria. It was created as a Soviet equivalent to the RAND corporation, which analyzed and sought resolutions for a range of global issues. Perhaps most importantly, the institute encouraged freedom of thought at unheard of levels at that time. There was virtually no censorship of ideology. I would venture to suggest that being able to work in such an unfettered atmosphere not only allowed A. A. Piontkovsky to flourish professionally and to feel part of a global scholarly community, it also fostered his freedom-loving way of thinking.

I have made a point to delve into Piontkovsky's academic background because it goes a long way to account for his profound knowledge and grasp of political processes; it also explains his ability to predict future developments both in Russia and across the globe.

For example, at the end of August 2014, Piontkovsky gave an interview to the radio station Nemetskaya Volna (DW) when he was the lead research scientist at the Institute for Systems Analysis. In the interview, he accurately described the drastic changes that took place in Kremlin policy and Russian society at large after Russia seized the Crimea:

> We entered a new phase of the so-called 'Russian World,' in my opinion, after Putin's speech in March [2014] at the Kremlin regarding the admission of new territorial units into the Russian Federation—namely Sevastopol and the Crimea. Here he spoke about the superiority and uniqueness of the Russian people's genetic code and its advanced levels of spiritual well-being. We are seeing the same acute manipulation of people's minds in Russia that we saw in the years of Nazism in Germany, this time coupled with a sophisticated tool—television broadcasts. . . . This ideology appeals to a person's basest and most sordid instincts—'We are Russians. We are better than everyone else.' The notion that the 'Russian world' is superior has essentially been used to justify the annexation of any piece of land with some percentage of Russian speakers.

Less than eight years later, Piontkovsky's predictions on where Russian society was headed came to pass in their entirety.

Piontkovsky, with the logical mind of a mathematician, saw clearly that Russia had passed a point of no return. He confidently foresaw the terrible war that a majority of politicians and political pundits doubted until the very last minute.

In the 1990s, not wanting to limit himself to his work at the institute, Piontkovsky began writing opinion pieces. He instantly made a name for himself. His political articles and essays are characterized by a depth of analysis matched only by his brilliant literary style. In this respect, Piontkovsky continues the tradition of Saltykov-Shchedrin. It came as no surprise when he was awarded the "Golden Gong-2001" in the international journalism category a mere three years after he published his first article.

The hundreds of pieces Piontkovsky has published both at home and abroad helped immensely to counter the Putin regime. It wasn't enough for him, however, to be a political writer. Unlike many of his fellow members in the intelligentsia, Piontkovsky did not regard politics as beneath him; he believed a good citizen should take an active role in the political sphere.

Piontkovsky tried to the very end to fight the Putin regime using legal methods. He was a member of the Yabloko party, the Solidarity movement, and the Steering Committee of the Russian opposition.

On March 10th, 2010, Piontkovsky and others composed and signed an appeal from the Russian opposition with the title "Putin Must Go."

Piontkovsky's active role in politics offered him an insider view of the so-called "mainstream opposition," which only deepened his skepticism towards the "liberals" in power. It became obvious to him that the Putin regime had stacked the deck in its favor and the "intelligentsia" was given a choice: do its bidding or play cards with a hustler. In their heart of hearts, they were relying not on themselves and their efforts but on some kind of miracle—a popular revolt, for example, a "black swan" event, or perhaps an unexpected softening in the manners and customs of the former KGB agents in power. They forgot one thing: there is no such thing as a former KGB agent.

I would be remiss if I did not cite two excerpts from Piontkovsky's articles on this topic:

> The most important of Andrei Dmitrievich Sakharov's principles has been forgotten—a sense of morality in politics. . . . By spurning Sakharov's legacy, the Russian intelligentsia basically committed moral and ideological suicide. It either joined the ranks of those in power or decided to do their bidding. ("In the Noose of Time," Feb. 12, 2009)
>
> Every one of the experts promoting these insane war discourses is from the societal group that considers itself "the best people in the country" or the "intellects of the nation." But it is this very group that bears the most responsibility for the catastrophe that took place in Russia at the beginning of the 21st century. ("The Banality of Evil," Aug. 24, 2016)

Piontkovsky is entirely his own man—beholden to no one. And so in many ways he has never been a clear fit for the Russian political landscape. In 2007, the Basmanny District Court in Moscow began hearing a case on whether to declare his book "An Unfavored Nation" extremist literature. In those times of yore, not all charges a prosecutor brought to trial resulted in an arrest, and Piontkovsky won the case.

Things changed in 2014 when the hybrid war with Ukraine began. In February 2016, the Prosecutor General's office found evidence of extremism in Piontkovsky's article "A Bomb Ready to Explode," published on the website of radio station "Echo of Moscow," and he was forced to flee the country.

But Piontkovsky continued writing from abroad, and established himself skillfully on the internet. His Youtube channel boasts hundreds of thousands of subscribers. He is a frequent guest on many of the opposition platforms on the web, and, most importantly, on official and unofficial Ukrainian media outlets. Today Piontkovsky reaches an audience of millions across the globe.

The subtitle of the book—"The Stakes of a Global War"—is very precise. For the last ten years, Ukraine has been waging a heroic war of liberation against an evil empire reborn. The outcome of this conflict will do a lot to determine the contours of the future global landscape. For me, for Piontkovsky, and for millions of others, a victory for Ukraine has been our life's work.

In 2021, the Ukrainian Cultural Studies Institution "Ï" awarded Piontkovsky a medal "For Intellectual Courage." But it emphasized that it was not "conferring" the award so much as asking the nominees to accept it as a sign of respect and gratitude—a recognition of how important the nominee is for the intellectual environment of Ukraine.

It is my feeling that the name of this award fully reflects the character of Andrei Andreyevich Piontkovsky.

His writings represent the irreproachable work of a man courageously devoted to defeating the evil of the 21st century.

Leonid Nevzlin
Philanthropist and Publisher

The Doomed City

First published on October 15th, 1999

The great Russian physiologist Ivan Pavlov, four years before his death in 1932, wrote, "I need to express my dismal view of Russian man—his brain system is so weak that he is incapable of perceiving reality for what it is. For him—there are only words. His conditioned reflexes are synchronized with words, not action."

Ivan Pavlov knew what he was writing about in 1932. Even Stalin could not have stated openly that the Russian peasantry needed to be eliminated, and even his most shameless propagandists could not bring themselves to trumpet such an agenda. But then the word peasant was replaced with the word "kulak." Suddenly leading figures of the Soviet intelligentsia—from Gorky to Sholokhov—began to nod their heads in approval as millions of these kulaks were relentlessly annihilated. A few years passed and these same conditioned reflexes, this time synchronized with the phrase "enemy of the people," compelled neighbor to inform on neighbor and demand that friends be shot.

A month has passed since the apartment building explosions in Moscow. The crime remains unsolved and investigators have not produced a single piece of evidence to link any one person or group of people of Chechen descent to the incident. But the word "Chechen" has already become a synonym for "terrorist" in the public consciousness; it is now firmly ensconced next to the verb "annihilate." And when one of us displays a moment of weakness and timidly inquires, for example, about the schools that were destroyed by the bombings and the children who were killed, the court dwarf dutifully appears on our television screens—the star of channel ORT. In a weary, patient tone of voice, he uses his prime-time slot to explain to those who have strayed that, strictly speaking, there are no schools in Chechnya in the generally accepted definition of the word. In Chechnya, you see, children are taught how to become terrorists and drug dealers. Therefore, their annihilation is not only morally justifiable but absolutely necessary.

One of the most astonishing publications to come out last week was a lengthy article written by the editor of "Nezavisimaya Gazeta," Vitaly Tretyakov (October 12, 1999). He addresses the nature of this most recent Chechen war and the attitudes of the "political elite" in more detail than anyone has to date. I should say he does more than address these issues; he lets the cat out of the bag, so to speak:

> It is patently obvious that the Chechens were lured into Dagestan and allowed to get bogged down so that there would be a legitimate reason to restore federal rule in the republic and to initiate a more active phase of the conflict to remove the terrorists assembled in Chechnya. This was clearly an operation conducted by the Russian intelligence services (do not confuse it with the apartment building explosions), and it was sanctioned at the very highest political levels.

Let's take another look at this text, one that could prove invaluable to historians, psychiatrists, and lawyers alike, as it cracks open a window into the sick consciousness of the Russian patient—"the Russian political elite." The author is not claiming a scoop here or editorializing; he speaks of this Russian intelligence operation that organized Basayev's incursion into Dagestan as if it were an indisputable fact, a fundamental truth fully understood by his well-informed readers. The scoop comes later, and reveals why Tretyakov wrote the article in the first place—you see, our patriotically inclined oligarch B also contributed his fair share to this brilliant operation.

And so, the "Russian political elite" has no problem with the fact that Basayev's incursion into Dagestan, which led to the deaths of hundreds of Russian soldiers, hundreds of Dagestani civilians, and the destruction of dozens of villages, was organized by the Russian intelligence services and was "sanctioned at the highest political levels." With only one goal: "to give Moscow a legitimate reason" to unleash a large-scale massacre in which thousands of Russian soldiers and tens of thousands of civilians would perish, just as in 1994–1996.

But if that is the case, what is the difference between, on the one hand, a president and prime minister who "sanctioned the operation at the highest levels" and an editor who proudly informs us about it, and, on the other, international terrorists and murderers such as Basayev and Khattab?

Incidentally, our editor, although fully occupied with the task of whitewashing his favorite oligarch, still manages to realize that he is perhaps revealing too much. Just in case, he hedges a bit by adding the parenthetical—(don't confuse it with the apartment building explosions).

And why shouldn't we confuse it? Both Basayev's incursion into Dagestan and the explosions in Moscow were used to reinforce the same straight-forward chain of conditioned reflexes in the public consciousness: "Chechen—terrorist—annihilate."

But it was the explosions in Moscow that truly reinforced this triad. And if presidents, oligarchs, and editors are capable, without batting an eye, of sacrificing hundreds of lives in Dagestan in the service of such absolute values as "geopolitical interests in the Caucasus," "consolidating the Russian elites," or the "grandeur of Russia," what's to stop them from conducting a similar redemptive sacrifice in Moscow?

A city with leaders like this, especially opinion leaders, is a Doomed City indeed.

Six Kilometers of Hell

First published on January 10th, 2000

A certain swindler, scorned and loathed by the entire nation but close to the extremely unpopular president's family, decided to take a road trip. He rode around the country trying to persuade governors to come together and form a new pro-Kremlin party a few months before the elections. He won over two or three that were mired in corruption scandals and one directly implicated in the murder of an opposition journalist.

A few months later, this "party" triumphed in the parliamentary elections. What exactly happened during these few months and how did this notorious swindler turn out to be so shrewd, investing money in what looked to be a hopeless endeavor?

Nothing much, really. Just Basayev's incursion into Dagestan (death toll: hundreds of Russian soldiers and hundreds of Dagestanis), the explosions in Moscow and Volgodonsk (approximately one thousand dead), massive bombings and a full-scale war in Chechnya (again, hundreds of soldiers dead. No one knows the exact figures, but a huge number of civilian casualties), and much more bloodshed and death to come.

On the plus side, however, we have our decisive alpha male in front of us on all the TV channels. He leads us from one victory to the next, dressed at times like the Prince of Wales in full military regalia, at times like a shogun from the Middle Ages in a kimono and a black belt. Our air power is "working over" Bamut while special forces conduct a follow-up "sweep" of Shali. These towns are straight out of the pages of Tolstoy's famous novel "Hadji Murat." How many more will we hear about in the three and a half months left in the presidential election campaign?

Three parties and three components of Putinism have created the government majority in the Duma. The corrupt governors, Zhirinovsky, and those masterminds of the Russian intelligentsia—the pro-Putin liberals. This last group finally achieved their goal of finding a Russian Pinochet who will use an iron first to promote "liberal reforms" and prosperity to the nation. And if thousands are murdered on the road to this better tomorrow, or, more likely, tens of thousands, oh well. As the swindler himself once said as he pioneered this new party of power, "so we're going to see some killing. People are always killing each other somewhere."

There are bad Chechens. They blew up our homes. The government repeats that line so often that it seems they are trying to convince themselves.

Then there are good Chechens whom we liberate from the bandits. The best and truest Chechen is the most pro-Russian one, Malik Saidullayev. He is the chairman of the State Council of Chechnya, elected to the position by Zavgaev's legitimate 1996 Supreme Soviet.

Malik Saidullayev on what happened after his native village was liberated from bandits: "Soldiers chased people out of the cellars where they were hiding. Some of them were carrying children in their arms—four or five years old. They lined them up and made them run six kilometers to the next village. They said only those who made it would be spared. Tanks then fired on them from behind as they ran."

There can be no doubt that there is Hell on Earth. We create it on a daily basis with our high-precision "Grad" and "Uragan" weapons. If Hell exists in Heaven as well, we can be sure to find in one of its recesses a six-kilometer field torn apart by projectiles. Chubais and his cronies will be forced to run through it for all eternity.

They will be forced to run through it, not Hero of Russia General Shamanov. There is no Hell for single-cell organisms. People like Shamanov are not guilty for they know not what they do.

Among those who celebrate this shameful, criminal massacre, calling it a Renewal for Russia and the Military, Chubais and his friends are the smartest, most educated, most high-profile, and most talented of them all. And the vilest as well.

Putinism as the Highest and Final Stage of Bandit Capitalism in Russia

First published on January 15th, 2000

The nature of Russia's socio-economic reality over the last ten years is not up for debate. Commentators ranging from Anpilov to Chubais in Russia and Soros to Summers abroad describe it in almost identical terms— buddy capitalism, family capitalism, oligarch capitalism, bandit capitalism. Choosing one epithet over another is really a matter of your personal taste in language. The essence of it does not change. The essence of the system entails total consolidation of personal wealth and power, to the point where the word "corruption" is no longer sufficient to describe the events taking place. Corruption in the traditional sense requires the existence of two parties—a businessman and a government bureaucrat whom the businessman bribes. Our Russian oligarchs (those like Potanin, Berezovsky, or Abramovich), however, don't need to waste their time or money on government bureaucrats. They themselves managed to become either high-ranking government figures or shadow advisers in the president's entourage who carry out administrative state functions. Boris Berezovsky openly announced this to the city and the world, with no lack of bombast, in his famous 1996 interview with *The Financial Times*. And thus, we witnessed the obscene coitus of money and power reach its logical conclusion.

The system achieved its present, permanent status after the 1996 Presidential Elections. To the horror of even some of its very creators, it has proven surprisingly resistant to any attempt to de-privatize the state. One of the key contributors to its creation was Anatoly Chubais. Let me remind you once again what he said after he stepped down from government: "In 1996,

I had to choose between the communists and bandit capitalism. I chose bandit capitalism."

Like many other reformers, Chubais believed it didn't matter how property was distributed; what mattered was creating a property owner. This property owner, it was thought, would "grow tired" of stealing and eventually start promoting efficient production. Only he won't do that. What has been privatized in Russia is not so much property as control over the flow of money, mainly the flow of government revenue. It is simply not possible for an efficient property owner to emerge when such a system is in place.

Like Frankenstein, reformers created their own monster—one of reform. This monster acquired a taste for unprecedented levels of personal enrichment, and, like a drug addict, will never be able to shake its addiction to appropriated funds.

After he himself appointed the super-rich to their positions, Anatoly Chubais naively hoped that he would eventually be able to introduce a new system, one with fair and transparent rules. The oligarchs' revenge was swift and merciless. Every one of their mass media outlets took aim at Chubais and sought to destroy his reputation. Unfortunately for him, they had no difficulty disclosing several incidents from his past which left him vulnerable to accusations of, at the very least, "conflicts of interest."

Evgeny Primakov and his government also attempted, albeit haltingly and inconsistently, to rein in the oligarchs, to pry them away from the government feeding trough and decision-making processes. These attempts were stopped just as decisively. The names of top-level oligarchs close to the throne may have changed: as one group lost influence (Smolensky and Vinogradov), another group rose to take their place (Abramovich and Askenenko). But all throughout, the essence of the system has remained the same. Its only concern for the year 2000 does not involve a sham computer virus; it involves the very real problem of how to conduct a national presidential election that only seems democratic.

The reliably privatized Boris Yeltsin could not run for a third term for a number of constitutional and health-related reasons. Even more significant was the fact that the very campaign model at play in 1996—using the threat of communism to frighten the electorate—was no longer effective. How long can you use Stalin's concentration camps to cover up your own thievery? They needed a fresh new ideology, and the intellectual lackeys were up to the task.

Feelings of disenchantment, aggravation and humiliation were widespread in the country, caused both by people's personal situation and the fact that Russia had obviously fallen far. These circumstances should have worked against the party in power. All the regime's strategists needed to do, however, was to channel all this frustrated energy to their advantage. An enemy was identified and a straightforward path proposed to achieve Russia's Renaissance. This time it was an ideology of patriotism that was stolen and "privatized."

Even the most hawkish proponents of the massacre in Chechnya have to admit that this is a war for the Kremlin, not for the Caucasus. More than anything else, it will ensure that power is inherited by the Yeltsin family's designated successor.

Where would presidential candidate Vladimir Putin's approval ratings stand today without the war in Chechnya? And would we have seen such massive support for the war or our outhouse killer-in-chief if there had been no mysterious explosions in Moscow at the very moment when the regime needed to inflame anti-Chechen hysteria?

Warfare is the primary instrument in Putin's PR campaign and everything else has been subordinated to it, even Boris Yeltsin's resignation.

If the puppet-masters are willing to take such measures as removing Yeltsin from office early to clear a path for Putin to be elected, they must be absolutely certain of his future loyalty. Such certainty can be guaranteed only by a deep knowledge of the candidate's professional and personal past.

It would be naïve to expect Putin to dismantle the system of bandit capitalism, grounded as it is in total consolidation of money and power. Many of the pivotal figures in the system are also the key shadow players behind the Putin project.

Putin's views on the economy are rather unclear; on the other hand, he often speaks enthusiastically about strengthening the role of government. As someone who has worked his entire life in law enforcement of some type, he seems to sincerely believe in this as some kind of panacea for resolving all economic woes. This view is incorrect even on the most general level. But in our case, when we have a government privatized by those seeking wealth and power, strengthening its role would be simply catastrophic. But that's enough about Putin. At the end of the day, he is the guy they found. If it hadn't been Putin, it would have been Poopkin. It's Putinism that's important, that is to say, the toolkit the regime uses to replicate itself.

Putinism is the highest and final stage of bandit capitalism in Russia. The stage when, as one semi-forgotten writer once said, the bourgeoisie tosses overboard the banner of democratic freedoms and human rights.

Putinism is waging war. It's "consolidating" the nation through hatred of an ethnic group. It's infringing on freedom of speech. It's information brainwashing. It's isolating from the rest of the world. It's further economic decline.

Putinism is—and here I'll use our acting president's favorite words—a confirm shot to Russia's head.

That's the legacy Boris Nikolaevich Hindenburg has left us.

The Spy Who Came into the Cold

First published on January 20th, 2000

At the beginning of January in the year 2000, a middle-aged man is standing somewhere in the middle of Chechnya. His face is one of a Russian peasant, ordinary and kind, not cruel. The kind of person you want to have a beer with or sit in the stands with and root for "Spartak." Or for the Central Sports Club of the Army. The man is the top Russian general in the Caucasus—Kazantsev. Let's hear what he has to say: "From now on we will consider only women, children under 10, and men over 60 to be civilians. We will deal with the rest in the harshest manner possible."

Comrade Stalin imprisoned peasant children for stealing corn if they were twelve or older. Comrade Putin will torment Chechen children in filtration camps starting at age ten, and not for stealing corn. And he will torment *them all.*

In light of current events, these measures are completely justifiable and even essential from a military point of view. And thus, we see how absurd the military point of view has become. At the dawn of the 21st century, we declare urbi et orbi that our fight is with a hostile and criminal ethnic group—the ubermensches of the Caucasus. Our Great Reich is in need of that parcel of land. And it must be cleansed of male Chechens older than ten.

"Why wasn't the *zachistka* (purge) conducted more efficiently?" the chorus of commentators asks indignantly on the leading TV channels. "We keep hearing 'Zachistka, zachistka, zachistka', when are we going to get a real one?" ask millions of Russians glued to their TV screens.

Come on—this particular zachistka was conducted a long time ago. It was a zachistka of your last remaining brain cells, my fellow citizens of this renewed Russia "rising from its knees."

People say that the poster boy for this Renewal is a diminutive lieutenant colonel; a universal soldier within the party, the KGB, the mayor's office of St. Petersburg, and the presidential administration. He brilliantly carried out all his bosses' tasks, including the procurement of "NATO secrets" for the Motherland from the Dresden House of Culture. He also navigated the financial jungle that is St. Petersburg, authenticated the genitalia of a disgraced general prosecutor, and wiped out Luzhkov and Primakov in the shithouse.

But now he has reached the cold, cold apex of power where no one gives him orders and there are no more bosses. He must feel uncomfortable, like an intelligence officer who has lost contact with headquarters.

This man who did incredibly well on all his atheism exams in college and in the KGB graduate program has suddenly become religious; he even dares to discuss theological matters in public, expounding on just why "our Saviour entered the world." He makes all effort to meet with church leaders, most likely hoping that he can use them to reestablish contact with headquarters.

But these church leaders can do nothing to help him. Their fear of him is genetic, almost chromosomal. He is too recognizable to them. It was his type—the unfailingly polite and tactful majors and lieutenant colonels with their cold, harsh eyes—that served as their handlers from the very beginning of their careers as clergymen.

He returns to the Kremlin and reads the casualty reports—the real reports, the ones unavailable to us. He remembers the words of Macbeth:

> *"For mine own good,*
> *All causes shall give way: I am in blood*
> *Stepp'd in so far that, should I wade no more,*
> *Returning were as tedious as go o'er."*

Apocalypse Now

First published on April 17th, 2000

Let's start with a quote from an article in "Nezavisimaya Gazeta," a publication that usually shows strong and consistent support for both Putin and the military operation underway in Chechnya:

> The massacre in Komsomolskoye lasted three weeks. Every imaginable weapon was used in the strikes, and some that were unimaginable. Every caliber of artillery was engaged. Combat vehicle guns and multiple rocket launchers did not let up for a moment. Surface-to-surface missiles were employed while helicopters and bomber planes dropped their payloads around the clock at a whirlwind pace ...
>
> Basements in the village were packed to the ceiling with the dead, their bodies mashed to a pulp. Corpses often consisted of nothing more than appendages; many had had their ears cut off.
>
> The stench at the cemetery is overwhelming. The wives, parents, and loved ones of the dead arrive from all over the republic in search of those missing. A mother identifies her son by a birthmark on his shoulder and embraces the corpse. The corpse has no face; it has been smashed in beyond recognition. The strange thing is: no one is crying. Although there are always hundreds of people here, an oppressive silence prevails. Four rows of graves stretch before your eyes for at least a hundred meters ("Nezavisimaya Gazeta," April 13, 2000).

"The strange things is: no one is crying." Let's remember those words. One hundred and fifty years ago, a Russian military officer said something similar after one of the many "purges." Perhaps a purge of this very village (although it was not called Komsomolskoye then):

> The village elders gathered in the square, squatted down, and discussed their situation. No one spoke of their hatred of the Russian military. To a man, the feelings of these Chechens ran deeper than simple hatred. It was not hatred; it was a complete refusal to recognize these Russian dogs as humans. When confronted with these entities and their grotesque cruelty, the Chechens reacted with disgust, revulsion, and bewilderment. Their desire to exterminate the Russians like one would exterminate rats, venomous spiders, or wolves was as natural a feeling as the feeling of self-preservation. (Lev Tolstoy, "Hadji-Murat," Chapter 17).

"No one spoke of their hatred of the Russians." This brief sentiment foresaw every Russo-Chechen war for the next 150 years. But we didn't listen.

"No one was crying at the cemetery. An oppressive silence prevails." And again we do not hear this silence. We will never conquer a people whose women refuse to cry at cemeteries. Even if we have convinced ourselves that this is a very bad people. All we can do is murder "all Chechen males over the age of ten."

We are told that Chechnya is not the main focus; the operation in Chechnya allows Russia to rise from its knees again—that's the goal. Russia's grandeur is now returning! It can finally begin pursuing its more ambitious goals and, in fifteen years, perhaps, be as successful as Portugal.

We have always built our shining cities—St. Petersburg, Belomorkanal—on top of bloodied corpses. The corpses of our own people. And after each and every "modernizing project," Russia plunged deeper into the slime pit of History.

Only this time we decided to erect our glorious, free-market Lisbon on a more solid foundation—someone else's bloody corpses stacked in the cellars of Komsomolskoye, Grozny, and dozens of other Chechen towns and villages. Apparently herein lies the essence of "enlightened patriotism," which our intellectual douchebags in government love to talk about.

Portugal need not worry. This is not how you rise from your knees. It's how you lose your ability to walk, and this time for good.

King and the President

First published on September 14th, 2000

Larry King's stock in trade closely resembles the art of recruitment. And so we can say that his interview with Vladimir Putin showcased two professionals going at it. But our lieutenant colonel from KGB foreign intelligence demonstrated far greater prowess than his interviewer.

Vladimir Ilyich Lenin, whose household staff included Putin's grandfather (he was either a cook or a valet), was fond of saying "Comrades, we are in need of useful bourgeois idiots." And thus, the almighty Larry King was subdued, converted, and molded into a useful bourgeois idiot.

Putin the operative was at his best when he offered up a different scenario for the demise of the Kursk: it had collided with an American submarine. His approach was subtle; with a few masterful brushstrokes, Putin sent his message to the viewer subconsciously, like a subliminal advertisement.

It was even more impressive that he managed to avoid linking himself personally to this manifestly false scenario: "Our submarines were involved in nineteen collisions. Nothing out of the ordinary. We just need to work out a general protocol for conduct at sea. I discussed this with my counterpart President Clinton."

The expected question concerning international assistance proved an easy one for Putin as well. He repeated the same fairy tale we heard when he met with the victims' families: assistance was only offered on the 15th of August and it was accepted immediately. But how was Larry King to know any of this. He can barely pronounce Russian last names—"Berryzovsky, Goozinsky." How was he to know that on August 16th Putin stood next to a man in Sochi named Kulibanov and this Kulibanov, the Chairman of the Emergency Commission to Rescue the Crew of the "Kursk" submarine, stated that he needed absolutely no foreign assistance.

Putin was equally adept in his answers to questions concerning human rights violations in Chechnya and alleged infringement of the freedom of the press in Russia. He deliberately chose his argumentation to align with Western values and frames of reference.

Chechen civilians have welcomed the liberating army with open arms and have even elected their own deputy to the Russian parliament. But Larry King's viewers will never know that this newly elected deputy, Alibek Aslanbekov, recently returned from a trip to Chechnya and was horrified by what he witnessed: major human rights abuses occur on a daily basis and people are arbitrarily arrested, murdered, tortured, and extorted.

They will never know that the Head of the Army in the North Caucasus has stated that he considers all "Chechen males over the age of ten and under the age of sixty" to be combatants. But then another general, a Hero of Russia, corrected this overly lenient colleague by saying that the wives and children of terrorists must be considered terrorists as well.

Putin's old chestnut about the little cross was used to great effect, too. A viewer in Russia would most likely react with derision to this poignant story, told for the tenth time at least (with some variation). Apparently after Putin's dacha burned down, a little cross was found intact among the smoldering ruins. It was later consecrated at the Holy Sepulchre in Jerusalem. But for regular church-goers in the United States, this story serves a purpose.

In my opinion, our professional made only one, barely noticeable, mistake over the course of the one-hour interview. It was the somewhat odd, self-satisfied smile on his face when he said, "It sank." (meaning the submarine).

The Larry King interview goes a long way in explain why politicians in the West are so taken with Putin. The "away game" Putin is quite a bit different from the one we see at home games. When he is traveling, he doesn't threaten to wipe anyone out "in the shithouse" and doesn't break down in self-incriminating hysterics while screaming "The media lies! The media lies! The media lies!" He also refrains from using vulgarities when he speaks to women (according to a transcript of a meeting on August 22, 2000 between Putin and the families of those who perished on the "Kursk" submarine). He lets himself act like this only when he is at home with his serfs.

And the serfs like it.

Thunderous, Prolonged Applause: All Rise (so they won't be sent to sit—in jail)

First published on November 20th 2003

Delegates from the 13th Congress for the Russian Union of Industrialists and Entrepreneurs greeted Vladimir Vladimirovich Putin with a truly sycophantic standing ovation, one rivaled, perhaps, in terms of its length and obsequiousness, only by the ovation given to Stalin himself by delegates from the 17th Congress of the All-Russian Communist Party (Bolsheviks).

In both cases, the delegates had more than enough reason to dislike the dour, diminutive figure on the podium whom they so enthusiastically applauded, but also enough reason to fear him quite seriously.

In both cases, the delegates decided to keep their hostility under wraps, for the last time in their political lives. Some delegates from the Congress of Victors cast several no-votes in the secret election of the General Secretary. The delegates from the Congress of the Vanquished reelected Mikhail Khodorkovsky to the Union's Board.

Both Congresses were essentially pointless and devoid of content; they did, however, represent a sort of symbolic shift in the post-revolutionary elite. In 1934, the shift was from Lenin's people to Stalin's. In 2003, from Yeltsin's to Putin's.

I'll admit that a shift in elites at the beginning of the 21st century will take place without the level of bloodshed seen in the first half of the 20th. Only a few will end up rotting in prison or mysteriously disappearing. Those who wish to will be allowed to emigrate. The Potanins and Kudrins will be allowed to keep some of their capital, a little property, and their concubines once they lay down their arms and swear an oath of personal fealty. But all in all, the Yeltsin elites (the senior oligarchs, the "liberal reformers," and the ideological lackeys of the regime) will depart the main stage without so much as a peep.

Innumerable studies have been devoted to the question: why did Lenin's people go so meekly to their death when faced with Stalinist repressions? And when put up against the wall, why did they continue to exclaim, "Long live Iosif Vissarionovich!"? At least some of these people had shown remarkable bravery during the Civil War and were certainly intelligent—they must have known perfectly well how events would turn out for them.

The key to the puzzle lies on the surface. The communist nomenclature could not oppose Stalin's dictatorship because this nomenclature had slowly but surely created it. It was fanatically loyal to it, completely comfortable operating within its framework, and worked hand-in-hand with it to commit crimes to include the annihilation of millions of Russian peasants during collectivization. Their fierce desire to remain within the system saw them applauding any and all repressions, including the execution of their own wives and brothers by firing squad. For them, Stalinism was not a rejection of Leninism. It was simply a logical and natural continuation of it.

This same mechanism works for the Yeltsin elites as well. Once they completed the process of privatization, a process viewed by the vast majority of Russians as unjust, they were unable to retain power and property by democratic means. A Russian Pinochet was needed, someone who would "guide Russian with an iron fist along the path of liberal reforms."

And so "Operation Successor" was launched in 1999, with the war in Chechnya serving as its main event and tool for success. The leading "liberals" tried to persuade us all that we would see "a new and improved Russian military" in Chechnya. They exuberantly compiled list after list of traitors who did not fall in line. Intellectuals obligingly developed ideological constructs such as "managed democracy," "authoritative modernization," "administrative vertical," and "dictatorship of the law." The same mechanism at work with Lenin's people will compel them to yell to the very end, "Long live the Empire! Long live Vladimir Vladimirovich!"

Putin Forever

First published on March 31st, 2004

The fact that the leader of Russia is named Vladimir Vladimirovich Putin is really a matter of happenstance. If it hadn't been for Boris Berezovsky and his desperate pushing, his name could very well could be Yury Mikhailovich or Evgeny Maksimovich.

What is much more important is that he sees himself as the bearer of a crucial, epic mission—the modernization of Russia. This process would allow us to draw even with the leading nations of the world and overtake not only Portugal but, dare I say, even the much more prosperous Luxembourg. The same motif has repeated itself now for centuries of Russian history—like Hegel's bad infinity. Over and over, a modernizing tsar appears on the scene, announcing urbi et orbi: "We are fifty years behind leading Western nations; if we do not embark on this new path, in ten or fifteen years we will be crushed." And it doesn't matter if it's Peter the Great or Joseph Stalin who utters the words.

With the nation's reins in one hand and a whip to flog those who doubt him in the other, the modernizer saddles up, lurches into the breach, and, as a rule, successfully completes his mission. At the cost of thousands of lives, he drags the country to the level of the seductive yet despised West, either in terms of the number of cannons and frigates or the amount of iron and steel produced per capita. And this then allows us to defeat the Swedes at Poltava, take over Paris and Berlin (several times), and be the first in space.

But for some reason, after every triumph of modernization, Russia ends up back where it started. A new leader takes over and feels compelled to tell the same old story: "We are lagging behind, we need to do this or that, Portugal, double our output or else . . ., etc."

What this means is that a systemic error has creeped into the bold projects we plan to modernize the country. There is something inherently different about the West, something our modernizers cannot grasp, that enables it to leave us in the dust again and again. And what do we have? Heap upon heap of iron and steel, countless decaying missiles and submarines, and facile dreams of a Third Rome and our special destiny, the details of which are confidential and held in a secret location.

When Peter the Great went to Amsterdam as a young emperor, he was humbled by the charms of Europe. He was taken in by everything—the magnificent shipyards, the clean sidewalks, the spectacular chocolate makers. And, of course, the reform-minded emperor immediately wanted to bring all of it back to Russia. But he wanted to do it in such a way that he could still behead the *streltsy* personally and, to take his mind off affairs of state, occasionally head down to the basement for some exercise. The exercise entailed using that aforementioned whip to flog his son for associating with foreigners without his permission.

Fast forward three hundred years to a young KGB officer arriving in Dresden, a committed party soldier devoted to his team. By this time, of course, thanks to the success of Russian modernizers, Dresden was not really the West. It had enough of the West in it, however, to serve as a kind of Future Shock for a spy just arriving from the East.

Whereas Peter, long interested in naval affairs, was most impressed by the shipyards in the Netherlands, Vladimir was bowled over by German beer. His musings on the subject of the local beer is the only memorable part of the rather boring "A Conversation with Vladimir Putin." Apparently the young officer was able to come to some important ideological conclusions about the doomed nature of the Soviet communist system thanks to this enticing, insatiably bourgeois beverage.

Thus, we can say that the now President Putin is completely sincere when he speaks of building a prosperous market economy in Russia "like the one they have in the West." But democracy has to be "managed" by Surkov, the "administrative vertical" customized by Sechin, and the "dictatorship of the law" governed by the human faces of Ustinov and Kolesnikov. And any oligarchs who disagree must be put in basement cells where they will write letters of repentance—"Koba, what do you need me to die for?" Those oligarchs who go along with it all will have to cough up millions. Liberal ministers will have to stand at attention and act like court jesters to amuse TV viewers at home while the governors portray themselves as loyal lap dogs.

The situation with the governors cannot be categorized as "back in the USSR." It's more like "back in 1580." The newest trend in political philosophy for the current Russian "elite," from Chuba to Chubais, is "I am your foul-smelling dog, my lord." (Ivan Vasilievich)

And that's essentially the systemic error made by all our exalted modernizers, an error repeated century after century. Charmed by the fruits of the West and overwhelmed by greed and a desire to possess them, our Scythian leaders look down their nose at the roots of Western civilization, at its atmosphere, that accursed atmosphere of Freedom and Human Dignity. And so we are left with Putin Forever, no matter what his last name ends up being in the next term.

The Road to Serfdom

First published on June 17th, 2005

Nearly two hundred years ago, one of our most distinguished fellow Russians, Peter Chadayev, advanced the idea that Russia's role in history is to serve as a kind of lesson to other nations. We show others what *not* to do under any circumstances. It certainly seems we have been eagerly, almost masochistically, playing this role to the hilt throughout these two hundred years. Another leading thinker of his time, the Austrian economist Friedrich von Hayek, is the author of the well-known book "Road to Serfdom," which identified two paths that lead to this outcome—fascism and communism. He could not have known when he was writing his work, however, that there would be another path, one that would lead people along it under the banner of von Hayek himself.

Vladimir Vladimirovich Putin has a bust of von Hayek displayed in one of his offices. One of its purposes is to attract foreign investors who sometimes visit the office. Vladimir Vladimirovich rather sincerely believes himself to be a liberal reformer. His advisors remind him of this constantly. His views on the economy in an odd but organic way combine elements of both Chubaisism and Chekism. And so I will henceforth refer to this philosophy, one that they espouse and actively implement, as the ChuChe model.

One of the most popular myths making the rounds these days is that there is a struggle going on within Putin's circle between two groups and their ideologies—the so-called liberals and the so-called *siloviki* (security forces). There is no ideological conflict whatsoever! The Russian political elites share the exact same morals and the exact same politics, which does not preclude skirmishes between discrete individuals or clans over who should control the financial streams.

Who are these *siloviki* or Chekists? Are they really against private ownership—that sacred cow of capitalism? Of course not. Perhaps they are against private ownership that isn't theirs, but that's about it. These people are very well-off and any friction between them and the classic Yeltsin-era oligarchs of late is simply a bunch of millionaires complaining about a bunch of billionaires.

And so who are these liberals then? It's Kudrin, Gref, Chubais, and their lot. People who have always wanted a Pinochet to call their own, someone who would use an iron fist to introduce "liberal" reforms to Russia. They have always been fine with the authoritarian nature of Russian elites.

By the way, which group do you support? The Yeltsin oligarchs or the Putin ones? It seems like Yeltsin's privatized more for themselves, but the Putin oligarchs are just starting out. It's just that with these more patriotically inclined ones around people have begun to disappear rather quickly. At least ten people have lost their lives and all of them were in one way or another involved in the "Three Whales" mystery. The key figure was shot while in a closely guarded room at the Ministry of Defense hospital. Yury Shchekochikhin was mysteriously poisoned and died in the Central Clinical Hospital in Moscow.

It's a tough call. I suppose it's a good thing we have a president whose entire career enables him to synthesize and combine both components of Russian capitalism. Putin really is Our Everything.

On the most general level, ChuChe puts into motion the golden plan of the Soviet KGB nomenclature that created perestroika in the mid-80s. What has it achieved after 20 years? A fully centralized political power base, much like the one we had before, immense personal fortunes which were inaccessible to them back then, and a completely different lifestyle (enjoyed by some in Courchevel, others in Sardinia). What's most important, however, is that they have rid themselves of any kind of social responsibility. They no longer have to regurgitate the party line—"The goal in life is to achieve happiness for ordinary people." Even back then this hypocrisy made them nauseated. Now they can say that the goal in life is "continuing to implement market reforms." And they will implement them with absolutely no regard for social consequences.

The long-held desire on the part of our "liberal" economists for a Russian Pinochet was frequently encouraged by several other countries where such a project was allegedly a success: Chile and several countries in East and Southeast Asia.

The problem with that is these countries used authoritarian methods to transition from an agrarian economy to an industrial one. Stalin used these same ruthless but effective methods 60-70 years ago. Europe as a whole industrialized in the 18th and 19th centuries using methods one could hardly call humane.

The issue facing Russia today—how best to transition to a post-industrial society—cannot be accomplished using these methods. This fact is proven if we look at these very same Asian "tigers" and "dragons" which our authoritarian liberals keep invoking. This model stopped working in South Korea back in the 1990s (many of the top leaders of Korean family-owned businesses as well as two former presidents of the country served lengthy prison terms). No, this model is in no way effective in moving to the post-industrial stage of a society's development.

And here in Russia we have an additional circumstance that complicates things even more: we are rich in raw materials and energy resources. This combination—an authoritarian government coupled with an abundance of natural resources—is simply devastating for a country's development. It separates the bureaucracy from reality, contaminating and corrupting it completely. That is exactly what is happening now. It's the classic mixture of a sedative and a laxative. The sedative is the price of oil—upwards of 50 dollars a barrel—and the laxative is the squad from Petersburg—those shapeshifting *siloviki*.

The result, therefore, is what you would expect. What I don't get is why Andrei Illarionov refers to this as the Venezuela disease. We are seeing a classic Russian tradition play out—a patriarchic government with chieftains collecting taxes. Whereas before, however, the sovereign and his bureaucrats were the sole owners of land and the puny people who worked on it, now the sovereign and his bureaucrats are striving to become the sole owners of a critical resource of the 21st century—oil and the puny people who pump it. And the rest of those puny people can be monetized completely.

The road that we are on is the third path to serfdom, and there won't be a fourth. Either the system will destroy the country or we will find the courage to take a different road. Then the entire Putin era will go down in history as a kind of final vaccine against the philosophy of serfdom.

The Unanswered Question

First published on September 9th, 2005

There are questions that countries avoid asking themselves, out of a sense of self-preservation, because they subconsciously know the answer. For example, who killed JFK or who was behind the explosions of those apartment buildings in Moscow and Volgodonsk. A well-articulated answer to these questions could prove disastrous for a country and so we never encounter one. And maybe that's for the best.

The question I am going to analyze today does not quite fit that category but remains a tough one nonetheless. It is so tough, in fact, that no one asked it directly at all last week during all the talk of Beslan, even during Putin's meeting with the mothers of the victims. It simply dissolved among all the other questions—about the number of hostages and the number of terrorists, the flamethrowers and tanks, the circumstances surrounding the first explosion, the chaos at headquarters, and so forth.

The question is the following: why was the option of asking Aslan Maskhadov (Akhmed Zakayev) to negotiate the release of the hostages discarded in favor of storming the school?

This question was first asked during the "Nord-Ost" theater tragedy. As a reminder—and this is very significant—the terrorists never demanded Mashkadov intervene as a negotiator during the hostage situations in "Nord-Ost" or Beslan—this was something our government initiated.

The terrorists' demands in both cases were more global, more vague; as such they were inherently unrealistic. The idea to give Maskhadov—a military adversary, an enemy—a chance to save our hostages would have signified an existential break with the vicious circle that doomed hundreds to their deaths. It would have moved the issue to an entirely different level.

During the "Nord-Ost" tragedy especially, this option would have not have resulted in the government losing face in any way. At the time, the official negotiators were Viktor Kazantsev and Akhmed Zakayev. They could have arranged for Maskhadov to intervene. Kazantsev and Zakayev met several times, including in Moscow.

High-level officials did meet for several hours and seriously discussed this option together with many other possible courses of action. Whether it could be implemented depended in large part on Victor Kazantsev, who was scheduled to arrive in Moscow in the morning. A different approach began to prevail during the night, however. Apparently, a group of *siloviki* managed to persuade Putin that the use of poisonous gas would not kill the hostages. And that if Maskhadov secured their release, he would gain a kind of legitimacy. The *siloviki* did not want this, and neither did a president who was now inextricably linked with "rubbing them out in the shithouse"—to a large degree a hostage to his own rhetoric.

And then we had an identical situation in Beslan. Before "Nord-Ost," Akhmed Zakayev was a legitimate partner in negotiations. By the time of the school siege, however, he had been declared a criminal, with Moscow working towards his extradition. And yet Zakayev was the one the Russian government turned to for help in getting the hostages released.

More Dangerous than an Enemy

First published on March 6th, 2006

The fundamental problem with the "elites" in the Russian government (and their gold reserves—the Petersburg crew) is that they need to conduct their thievery here, in Russia, but then spend their ill-gotten gains and enjoy the discreet charms of bourgeois consumption over there—in the West. Not in North Korea, of course, or in Iran or Belarus. And thus, we can observe a certain cognitive dissonance within the elite's perception of the outside world.

For domestic consumption, the country is likened to a fortress under siege. The West, the US, the global powers that be—all aspire to deprive Russia of its sovereignty and then dismember and destroy it. Decrying an enemy, an external threat, is the only way the ruling elites can ideologically justify staying in power. That is the only task they have set for themselves. Unlike previous regimes, they do not promote building communism, or overtaking Portugal, or doubling the GDP.

In the gangster slang of the Petersburg crew, "We will not permit anyone to deprive Russia of its sovereignty" means "we will permit anyone to pry us away from the government feeding trough."

But there is a second, no less important, component to the task. They also need to whitewash both themselves and their loved ones in that same West they so despise and make sure their memberships in its prestigious clubs—from the G8 to, I don't know, the Amateur Elephant Hunters of Central Africa—remain intact. To achieve these goals, enormous sums of money are allocated using a section of law almost mockingly entitled, "Promoting a Positive Image of Russia Abroad."

The biggest threat to the prosperity of the brigade's top leadership would be if they were personally accused of corruption. Therefore, a huge amount of time and money are spent on propaganda directed at countering any such claims. "Operation Schroder" marked the first major tactical success in this area.

By transforming the leader of a major European power into "just one of the guys" from Petersburg, the entire crew, or its "inner circle" at least, managed to join the global club of the chosen, out of the reach of all those whack-job Swiss prosecutors.

"Operation Evans" was initiated to conduct a thorough and decisive whitewashing of the Petersburg crew. The former US Secretary of Commerce and personal friend of the president found it within himself to refuse after two weeks (!) of indecision. But he was definitely tempted. Who wouldn't be when offered a five-year contract and a 40 million USD annual salary?

There are several top-level Putin apologists in the West. Besides Schroder and this Evans who changed his mind at the last minute, there is also Berlusconi, especially if he loses the election. There is also a middle level comprised of prominent analysts and experts whose job it is to put a positive spin in the West on the corruption phenomenon among Russian leaders without damaging their professional reputation as writers.

But all this is very complicated, as one famous political strategist put it, especially if we recall when the Petersburg crew seized "Yukos," the thirteen trillion-dollar deal between Abramovich and Putin for "Sibneft," and, finally, Putin's sensational admission the other day that the fictious company "Baikalfinansgrup" was created for one purpose only—to handicap any possible legal challenges to the seizing of property from the original owner.

Let's see how our friend Anatole Lieven deals with all this. Lieven published an article this week in the Financial Times with the mournful title "Do Not Condemn Putin out of Hand."

It is full of the hackneyed pseudo-arguments we have heard a thousand times from Mark Pavlovksy to justify the Putin regime. But the arguments are not what arouse interest—it's the innovative approach the author takes in addressing the most controversial topic for a customer corruption at the highest levels of the Russian government. The key sentiment here is so remarkable that it needs to be reproduced in the language of Shakespeare and, of course, Anatole Lieven—"The new Russian elite of Mr. Putin's conception . . . will move freely between the state and market sectors, and in the process will be handsomely rewarded; but it will keep its money within Russia, not spend it on British football clubs or French chateaux."

You can die now, Anatole! You won't top that![1] Hurry up and take your work directly to the prosecutor's office in Russia and in Switzerland and to the Nobel Committee as well. Tell them you have produced the best definition of corruption the world has ever seen.

But the always obsequious Anatole must realize on some level that he is revealing too much. Instead of a period he uses a semicolon and finishes on a note of high patriotism: "But it will keep its money within Russia, not spend it on British football clubs or French chateaux."

It's a weak caveat, let's be honest. First of all, the details regarding a thief's personal consumer spending and the location of his ill-gotten gains do nothing to mitigate his guilt. Secondly, the most prominent example of "the new Russian elite of Mr. Putin's conception," someone who moves freely between the federal and private sectors and is handsomely rewarded as he does so, is Roman Arkadievich Abramovich. Abramovich is a Russian governor, one of the richest men in Russia, a personal friend and business partner of the president, and, perhaps most importantly, someone who aided Putin in his rise to power. And he actually *does* spend his stolen money on English football clubs and French chateaux. So, our friend Lieven is simply lying through his teeth and hoping his readers in the West aren't informed enough to realize it.

Still, the first part of the sentence is worth a lot. Maybe fifteen years each for this "new Russian elite of Mr. Putin's conception." See how an obsequious idiot is more dangerous than an enemy?

---

1   A paraphrased version of Grigory Potemkin's statement to Denis Fonvizin after attending the premiere of Fonvizin's play, "Nedorosl'"—"You can die now, Denis! You won't top this!"

At the Window to Europe

First published on June 27th, 2006

Russia and the West are yet again giving up on each other. This dance of attraction and repulsion has gone on for many centuries, with this latest repulsion phase making one look at things philosophically. Historians have recorded more than twenty-five of these cycles dating back to the reign of Ivan III.

In its post-Soviet incarnation, Russia has already passed through two of these shifts. Under Yeltsin, we had a shift from Kozyrev to Primakov, while in our current regime we witnessed the 9/11 Putin with his "Americans, we are with you" shift to the Putin we have today. This Putin claims that Islamic terrorists in the Caucasus are "a mere tool in the hands of Russia's traditional enemies. They are more experienced, more powerful, and strive to weaken us and tear us apart." He also threatens the US about every two months with strikes from state-of-the-art missiles developed by Russian scientists (all the while accepting money from those same Americans to maintain the security of the Russian nuclear arsenal). Wait, there's more. Putin is doing all he can to remove American military bases from Central Asia even though a NATO defeat in Afghanistan would open up a corridor to Russia for Islamic terrorists via Central Asia and the Caucasus.

What dangers are posed by this latest anti-Western shift on the part of the Russian political class and its illustrious mediocrities?

First and foremost, the shift is occurring at a time when the West and Russia are no longer the absolute dominant players on the world stage as they were in the 19th and 20th centuries. Both the West and (especially) Russia have never been more vulnerable. They have never been faced with such fundamental, almost existential, challenges. Russia and the West have never needed one another more and cannot risk a breakdown in relations.

At the same time, though, the causes of this latest sharp foreign policy U-turn that Russia has made in its attitude towards the West are not relenting as they have many times before as the pendulum begins to swing back.

On the contrary, in light of specific historical circumstances, these causes are experiencing a synergetic self-evolution and there are at least four of them.

Let's start with the trauma caused by Russia losing the Cold War, its empire, and its status as a superpower. This trauma gave rise to a deep-seated and enduring psychological complex within the collective subconscious of the Russian political class. The West has remained a spectral adversary for them, an enemy that gives meaning to their existence. All the myths perpetuated by Russian foreign policy makers have been and always will be grounded in our nation's heroic opposition to the West.

Long into Putin's forced retirement and removal from government, he will curse his con artist speechwriter for rewriting the Sudetenland "good Hitler" speech in time for his Crimea performance on March 18th. No one should open graves such as these.

A people who defeated Nazism in Germany and then turned this victory into a kind of pagan cult is now eagerly slurping up every ideological tenet of Nazi pornopropaganda. The difference this time is the propaganda is multiplied ten-fold thanks to modern-day media—a people in decay, the collecting of German (Russian) lands, the Third Reich, (the Russian World, the Fifth Empire) Ein Volk ein Reich ein Fuhrer, a bunch of traitors to the state.

It's as if it's August 2, 1914 all over again, with the entire country on its knees in front of the palace in Novo-Ogaryovo with their flags and their banners and their St. George ribbons, their icons and their portraits of the tsar.

The stern proletarian leaders of the Left Front, convicted of organizing an insurrection on the sovereign Emperor's inauguration day, howled in loyal unison from their gloomy dungeons: "Long Live Vladimir Vladimirovich Putin, the Collector of Russian lands!"

The bourgeois opposition ladies flirtatiously toss bouquets of exquisite compliments at the feet of the macho Collector. The only thing missing were those classic words: "A pure Aryan who shows no mercy when dealing with the enemies of the Russian World." The words were uttered a few days later by a remarkable Russian patriot and esteemed grandson of Molotov-Ribbentrop, declaring Putin, himself, and all the rest of us the descendants of an Aryan tribe that descended from the Carpathian Mountains and peacefully populated the Eurasian lands all the way to Fort Ross on the Pacific Ocean.

The leader had not expected such a clamorous response and had had no intention of producing one. He had set before himself one specific, pragmatic task: to sodomize Ukraine like only a brother can and prevent it from escaping the Eurasian network of mafia crime bosses in favor of a European model of economic and political competition. Such a model would have proved a dangerous temptation for Russian society and undermined the spiritual foundation of thievery on which our Judofuckery of a government is based. The annexation of Crimea was simply a way to resolve the Ukraine issue and nothing more; it was not meant to launch a campaign of spiritual renewal for the Russian World. Before the 18th of March, Putin had not given a thought to Vladimir Tavrichesky's historic mission to amass and conquer more Russian lands. He would have been perfectly satisfied with being praised for a much more minor accomplishment—suppressing the Ukrainian anti-mafia revolution. But after March 18th he fell hostage to a new heroic myth, a myth that soon won the hearts of impressionable Russians and instantly wiped from their collective memory the increasingly popular memes shouting "Putin is a thief!"

And then we got a new slogan, one to replace the one from 1999. Remember? It was inspirational at first but then became somewhat hackneyed: "Rub them out in the shithouse." The new one—"The Collector of Russian Lands"—is a fresh and effective foundation for mythmaking and will go a long way to legitimize Putin's desire to remain in power for life. He is now Our Everything; he's Ivan the First, Dmitry Donskoy, Ivan the Terrible, Peter the Great, Catherine the Great, and Joseph the Bloody all rolled into one. Crimea is Ours (*Krymnash*). The Russian World. This romantic remake of a myth-making system is useful for a leader for a number of reasons, not the least of which is that it assumes the existence of external enemies and traitors to the state. It also provides a simple and lasting justification for the need to purge any opposition leaders in the harshest manner possible. In point of fact, Putin is not capable of formulating a policy proposal that would cement his grip on power. But there is still some risk involved with his chosen method. It requires a certain amount of dynamism, a constant expansion of the "Russian World" universe. For an ideology such as this one, the status quo or even a whiff of retreat in the face of our enemies would prove fatal. It would arouse the deepest of suspicions even among the regime's most ardent supporters. The suspicion that "Our tsar is not the Real One!" And so now Putin is destined to be "Vladimir the Real" until his last day in power, pandering all the while to his Aryan tribe descended from on high.

And then we have the West. The West that is so self-satisfied, so hedo-nistic, decadent, bureaucratic, lazy, deceitful, cowardly, hypocritical, and cyn-ical. But our Aryan tribe has for centuries been unable to avert its slanted gaze from the place, a gaze filled with equal parts hate and love. The West in ques-tion offered Putin a Munich-Geneva deal: We'll forget about Crimea and the rest of Ukraine can remain an independent, non-aligned nation within your sphere of influence, akin to Finland under the Soviet Union.

Before March 18th, Putin would have agreed to this, albeit after negoti-ating for himself the strictest possible parameters for governing this remain-ing Ukrainian territory. And then he would have put an end to the matter filled with a sense of deep satisfaction. But Putin after March 18th was not the same man. By then he had discovered a personal Holy Grail to ensure his immortality!

During this year's April 17th Direct Line press-conference with his fellow tribesmen, Putin made a point to try and raise our spirits by pointing out that we all are carriers of a unique genetic code. With his usual magna-nimity, he listed several other tribes and nations and the qualities we often see in them (opportunism and materialism, for example). But he placed great emphasis on his view that we are fundamentally superior to all other nation-alities: *They don't have a f-cking ounce of spirituality.* To conclude, he assigned a new, inspired task to our breathless tribe—Novorossiya: six Russian oblasts illegally granted to Ukraine by the Bolsheviks.

The godless and spiritless West became somewhat puzzled by all of this. After all, it had always been willing to give up Ukraine. Some of the first reactions in the West on the Ukraine crisis came from Obama and Rasmussen who stated that the US and NATO had absolutely no intention to intervene militarily in the conflict seeing that Ukraine was not part of the alliance. Indeed, who would go to war with a nuclear superpower on behalf of a country that it had no obligation to defend? Forget about the Budapest Memorandum—it's about as useful as a blank piece of paper. A chicken is not a bird and a memorandum is not a treaty. Putin's subtle threat of nuclear war worked well in the case of Ukraine, but it put serious pressure on our official partners. What was next? Crimea? Novorossiya? What else were they going to have to sacrifice on the ghostly altar of this Aryan tribe, a tribe that has been rising from its knees for two decades and doesn't seem to know how to make itself useful? Would it be Northern Kazakhstan? Putin plays the role of a crazy person, that's part of his job and his strategy, but the man knows what he is doing. He knows perfectly well that all he needs to do is mention these territories in passing in the context of the grand Russian World ideology and Zhetysu[2] will be flooded with polite little yellow men. There will be a lot of them, and they will block the Trans-Siberian Railway and encourage the native peoples in the Far East to express their intent to reintegrate with their historic Motherland—the Yuan Dynasty. And it's useless to count on nuclear weapons when you're fighting a civilization which has absolutely no regard for human life. So what remains to support the resilience of a Collector of Russian Lands ideology?

The answer is Narva. A *Russian* Narva. This is a city that has seen the glory of Russia. A Danish fortress burned to the ground by Ivan the Terrible that for some strange reason is now located on the territory of a NATO aggressor member state. If we compare, however, the number of conventional weapons NATO has with the number the Russian World possesses at the moment, it's clear that no matter how many little green men are sent to Narva and how much equipment they have with them to carry out a referendum to join Russia, NATO aggressor forces could wipe them out in half an hour.

But they won't be wiped out, because they have the support of the one who sent them, the semi-insane (or so the West thinks) leader of the Russian World with one of the largest nuclear arsenals in the world at his disposal. So much more than that nuclear garbage that Kim Jong Un has. If his forces are defeated after invading, a deeply vulnerable Putin will not resort to mutually guaranteed suicide with the United States, at least at first. Instead, he will threaten to destroy one or two major European cities. And what will we hear from the US in response? People such as Dmitry Konstantinovich Simes, a respected statesman and former Soviet intelligence operative, as well as Henry Kissinger, that stalwart of American diplomacy, will ask the same question: "Do you want to die for Narva?"

The fact of the matter remains that the West will never go to war with Russia to protect Estonia (or Latvia), much like it didn't go to war to protect Ukraine. The Kremlin fully understands this and is gleefully weighing the appetizing opportunities these circumstances present.

---

2   Southeastern Kazakhstan —Transl.

Putin is a keen observer of his Western counterparts and has nothing but contempt for them. How else should he look upon these great heads of state of Europe when all they do is line up like sycophants at his gas pumps for a sad two million Euros a year? And let's not forget that Putin and Assad made Western leaders look like fools with one chemical strike; they changed the course of the crisis in Syria completely. Suddenly, Assad was no longer just a run-of-the-mill murderer responsible for the destruction of the Sunni community; he was now viewed by the global community as a respectable actor on the world stage engaged in the noble cause of chemical weapon disarmament. Putin saw right through Obama and his red lines back then just as he sees through his former G8 partners today. He knew he'd be able to outmaneuver them in any potential military conflict that might arise on the path to fulfilling the grand Russian World ideology, and he could do it without so much as unsheathing his sword. This despite the reality that NATO has a much larger conventional arms arsenal than Russia as well as superior nuclear capabilities. We will prevail, the thinking goes, by virtue of our spirit. Our spirit and our insolence.

But it seems the Kremlin underestimates the other side of this dilemma that is so painful for the West. The US cannot afford to ignore its obligation to defend the territory of a NATO member state. A refusal to defend Narva would signify the end of the NATO alliance, the end of the US as a world power and its departure from the pages of history. Is there no way the US can resolve this conundrum?

There is a way, and it involves preventing, on a fundamental level, the unsolvable Narva scenario from ever developing. Putin has mined the last century for an ideology that is both insane and extremely dangerous for Russia and the world at large: the collecting of "ancestral lands." The world must prove (first and foremost to Russian society) that this ideology is unsustainable and it must do so at the earliest (Ukrainian) stage of its development. The West has the capability to accomplish this through more and more severe sanctions, including those targeting discrete individuals. It's true that sanctions don't just hurt Russia; they have a negative effect on the global economy as well. But as of March 18th, 2014, **Putin has become an existential problem for the West**, and solving this problem is going to come at a cost.

In addition to these sanctions, the citizens of Russia and the world at large deserve a detailed report on the ins and outs of Putin's personal wealth and financial assets as well as those of his close associates. Disclosing this information to the public would be a more significant political threat to

Putin than simply freezing his accounts. The fallout from such a disclosure would make it very difficult for the spiritual leader of the Russian World to successfully continue his historic mission—his subjects would learn that this celebrated collector of Russian lands is also a fervent collector of the American dollar.

Who Killed Anna Politkovskaya

First published on October 16th, 2006

Fascists have killed Anna Politkovskaya. She has been murdered by the same gang that three years ago poisoned another contributor to *Novaya Gazeta*, Yury Shchekochikhin. At that time those star-spangled FSB generals were still just petty thieves extorting protection money from furniture stores, without any particular ideological fig leaf.

They got away with the murder of Shchekochikhin and of many others. They became emboldened, acquired a taste for it, and the most enterprising of them, who by now were asset-stripping oil and gas companies, broke through into the charmed circle of the world's richest people.

In order to maintain themselves on this vertiginous peak in a country one third of whose population lives below the poverty line, they need to fool the people, to point the finger at "enemies of the nation"—the West, people from the Caucasus, and other non-Russian peoples living in Russia, the few journalists still intrepid enough to criticize the Putin regime.

People are puzzled by the excesses of the campaign against Georgia, openly and energetically fanned personally by our head of state. From a geopolitical point of view it is counterproductive. Ethnic purges in the streets of Moscow irretrievably undermine Russia's authority as a great state and will sour relations—not only with Georgia, but also with all our neighbors, for a long time to come.

On the other hand, these tactics appeal to the worst instincts of the mob and make it a significant force supporting the regime.

Our head of state, a lawyer by training, has introduced a new term— "the native people," to which he contrasts "semi-gangster groupings that are sometimes also ethnically tinted."

It would be difficult to make a more blatant appeal for racial attacks in a country already riven with ethnic divisions. Russia's most active neo-Nazi organization, the Movement Against Illegal Immigration, promptly paid enthusiastic homage to Russian President Vladimir Putin, seeing him as its ideological leader.

That Nazi, Alexander Dugin, who makes no secret of his infatuation with the aesthetic and practice of Hitler's SS, is never off the screen of the state television stations, having now been promoted to the position of one of the leading official ideologists of the regime.

The last document with the signature of Anna Politkovskaya was an appeal to society and the state authorities to "Stop the Persecution of Georgia." I am proud of the fact that my signature is alongside hers.

Ms. Politkovskaya knew that she was doomed in Putin's Russia, and spoke about this on more than one occasion. Her revelations about the massive violations of human rights in Chechnya, which continue to this day, about the shameful behavior of the state authorities during the catastrophic hostage-takings of the audience of the Nord-Ost musical in Moscow and of schoolchildren and their teachers and parents in Beslan, were a red flag to the regime. There had already been more than one attempt to kill her.

It is symbolic, and was almost predictable, that she should be murdered in these dog days of the repulsive xenophobic bacchanalia that has seized Russia. This is a time when everybody, the human trash in the streets, the intellectual menials of the regime, has received from the "demons" ensconced in the Kremlin what Dostoyevsky called, "a dispensation to be dishonorable." Some of those particularly inebriated by this right evidently decided to celebrate the birthday of their beloved president in their own way.

We have lost our most honorable, intrepid and talented colleague. What next? Go to the neo-Nazi Web site, www.russianwill.org/ material/ vragi.html, which has existed unhindered on the Internet for many years now. You will find there photographs and home addresses of those they have condemned to death, and a call to carry out the sentence. Sergey Kovalyov, Svetlana Gannushkina . . . there is a long list of names. They are the most honest and conscientious people in Russia. Will their turn be next?

I do not know. In the absence of free speech and effective democratic institutions, a growing responsibility rests on "intellectuals" who are today still collaborating with the regime. Will they continue to watch as our country slides toward Chekist fascism, or will they have the courage to say "no?"

A particularly disreputable role in abetting Russia's descent has been played by the "statesmen" who are said to lead "democratic countries of the West." They have known the answer to the famous question, "Who is

Mr. Putin?" for a long time now. Anna Politkovskaya (among many others) warned them who they were dealing with. Her books have been translated both into English and French and have been widely reviewed.

But some of them want to participate in exploiting the Shtokman gas condensate deposit in the Barents Sea. Others seek Russian votes in the UN Security Council. And, so, they carry on pretending that Putin is a respected member of the club—their club—and one of them. And worst of all, it may be true.

From Russia with Death

First published on November 27th, 2006

The diabolical professional sophistication evident in the poisoning of Alexander Litvinenko makes it absolutely clear that this was not the work of amateurs.

This leaves only two logical possibilities: journalist Anna Politkovskaya and Alexander Litvinenko were flagrantly murdered in the center of Moscow and in the center of London for purposes of intimidation by the Russian intelligence services on orders of the president of Russia, or they were "liquidated" by breakaway groups within the intelligence services that are engaged in a merciless power struggle within the Kremlin.

If it is the first case, fascism has already triumphed; the situation portrayed in Vladimir Sorokin's novel, "Day of the Oprichnik," is already here; and all of us for whom such a regime is ethically unacceptable and aesthetically repugnant are going to be killed with varying degrees of brutality no matter what we now do or say.

So let us look at the second possibility, no matter how improbable it may seem. This scenario suggests that Chekist fascism is barging its way to power and that the only obstacle in its path is a president who does not want to wreck the Russian constitution and find himself marooned indefinitely in the Kremlin as its puppet.

It would be entirely reasonable to comment that, even so, President Vladimir Putin bears moral and political responsibility for the situation that has developed, and to scornfully denounce those gangsters fighting it out in the Kremlin that have been maddened by all the oil and gas billions they have gotten their hands on. That would oblige us to revert to scenario No. 1.

However, it seems that there is still a chance to save our country. But for this we will need an exceptionally broad coalition of politically active citizens rallying to the defense of the present constitution. We will also need a legally elected president who enjoys the trust of the majority of the Russian population.

We will need something else: The political will of the president himself and his readiness to put his trust in this coalition and in the belief that the Russian people have in him. Only if he will do that has he any prospect of facing down forces that he is evidently no longer able to control within the top-down structure of the "administrative vertical" that he and his ever-obliging political advisers have created.

By a broad coalition I mean more than those parties that are traditionally classed as "democratic" and "liberal" and that have representatives in the Civic Chamber; more even than the opposition parties on the left. In today's highly volatile situation, the success of an anti-fascist coalition requires also the participation of a significant section of the "party of government"—people who are loyal to Vladimir Putin but who are not prepared to accept that the intelligence services should be unaccountable and unchallengeable. It requires the involvement of a business community that wants to be free to work in Russia and not constantly to feel under threat. It needs to include those civil servants in the bureaucracy who retain a sense of responsibility for the welfare of the state, as well as many leading figures in the mass media.

The viewpoint of people like these was persuasively articulated about a year ago in the renowned "Letter to the Congress" signed by eighteen prominent members of the ruling United Russia party. They specifically warned at that time that "the security ministries and services are becoming an independent political force." The letter was hushed up, and its authors and their like-minded colleagues opted for a behind-the-scenes struggle rather than defending their political views in public. They redirected their energies into the dead-end policy of trying to come up with a "liberal successor."

It should be clear to them by now that in any behind-the-scenes struggle they are going to be the losers. Only by coming out openly into the political arena do they have any chance of attracting broad public support, as well as allies in the numbers they need from those who are today in opposition.

What should the political platform of this coalition be?

First, it should demand an investigation, as transparent as possible, into all the political murders of recent years, beginning with the poisoning of Duma Deputy Yury Shchekochikhin. These investigations must culminate in the severe punishment of the guilty. As regards the murder of Yury Shchekochikhin, the investigation has progressed well enough but has ground to a halt just as it was becoming clear that the suspects include those in charge of the FSB, Russia's state security services.

Second, it should require the removal from their duties, before the end of the investigation, of those top figures in the intelligence services that could adversely affect its outcome.

Third, it should insist that the disgraceful word "successor" be expunged from the vocabulary of Russian politics. The search for a "suitable" successor implies shameful guarantees of immunity from prosecution to the departing president. The best guarantee of the personal, political and historical future standing of Mr. Putin would be his handing over of power on May 8, 2008 not to some successor spawned by court intrigues, but to a new president of Russia chosen in transparently fair and free elections.

Fourth, this coalition should campaign for the abolition of nearly all of the recent innovations in electoral legislation designed to undermine democracy, and for the provision to all political groups, which respect the Constitution of the Russian Federation, of equal opportunities to participate in the parliamentary elections in 2007 and the presidential elections of 2008.

How can we bring together this coalition of patriotic forces in the immediate future (before the next murder)?

It is essential to persuade those colleagues within the party of government who share our aims that they need to come out openly into the public political arena and fight for our goals, addressing their appeal to the country and not solely to the president, who is surrounded by an impenetrable ring of security officials.

The debating of questions that vitally affect Russia's future must be brought out of the dark recesses of the Kremlin. Dark recesses breed rats.

Saving Lt. Col. Putin

First published on December 4th, 2006

I warned in my recent column for Insight, "From Russia with Death," that very little time remains before the next murder takes place. I did not then know that a (fortunately unsuccessful) attempt had already been made on the life of former Russian Prime Minister Yegor Gaidar.

The current little "joke" in Moscow is, "Not everybody is going to see in the New Year." Since that is very soon, I return to some of the points in my article, which has stirred up a raging controversy both in Russia and in America.

First, as regards my own attitude to Russian President Vladimir Putin: It has not changed. It remains just as negative as it was when, at the beginning of the effort to find a replacement for Boris Yeltsin, Mr. Putin first monopolized our television screens, winning the hearts of the nation with his plebeian slang.

However, there has never been anything personal in my attitude toward the man. It has been based solely on the extent to which Mr. Putin could bring good or evil to Russia.

Thus, I publicly supported him in 2001 when, against the prevailing opinion of his entourage, he spoke out as an ally of the United States in the Afghanistan operation and, without the loss of a single Russian soldier's life, resolved an important issue of the country's security: how to liquidate a bridgehead for Islamist radicals, who were preparing to move on Central Asia. For the first time in Russia's military history, somebody else did our dirty work for us. Usually, the reverse has been true.

Right now Mr. Putin finds himself in a situation in which, as the end of his second term approaches, he can again play a positive role in Russian history.

Within Russia and beyond its frontiers, assassinations and attempted assassinations are taking place of "enemies of the people," lists of whom are to be found on all our country's quasi-fascist websites. It is only going to be possible to continue blaming these murders on the CIA, or the oligarchs

Boris Berezovsky (in Great Britain) or Leonid Nevzlin (in Israel), for a few more days, until the British, as seems likely, publicly and officially produce compelling evidence showing that the tracks of Alexander Litvinenko's murderers lead straight back to Moscow. The president of the Russian Federation will then have to make possibly the most momentous decision of his life.

Much the same dilemma faced the one-time President of Poland, Wojciech Jaruszelski, when his intelligence services brutally murdered their own "enemy of the Polish people," Father Jerzy Popieluszko. Mr. Jaruszelski could have tried to cover up the crime, thereby irrevocably becoming an accomplice (and if he had, he would undoubtedly be in prison today). Instead, he chose to hand the murderers over to justice and as a result has remained, even today in post-Communist Poland, a respected political figure.

More important, however, than the fate of the Russian president is the fate of his country. The effective legitimization of these serial political murders will make not only Mr. Putin but all of us hostages of the institutions which are committing them. That is quite apart from the fact that Russia's international reputation for years to come depends on whether a radiological attack on a G8 partner was sanctioned by the head of the Russian state rather than by some rabid FSB oil baron.

We have to help the president of the Russian Federation to come to the right decision. He is, of course, unlikely to listen to the voices of his opponents. That is why what is needed is a broad coalition of supporters of Mr. Putin, of that section of United Russia, the party of the government, which, if only from the instinct of self-preservation, will be prepared openly to speak out against a creeping destruction of the Russian constitution which is tantamount to a coup d'état.

To judge by several signals from the Kremlin, Mr. Putin is wavering. Some sound advice from his partners in the G8 to their friend Vladimir could play a crucial role.

It is pointless for those partners to speculate on the extent to which Mr. Putin is personally involved in these crimes. That never comes to light in political assassinations. In medieval England, King Henry II once gave vent to his frustration at his political opponent, Thomas a Becket, the Archbishop of Canterbury. Four of the king's knights fell upon the leader of the Church in England and, to use Mr. Putin's phrase, "wiped him out in the shithouse." Historians argue to this day over whether the king intended his comments as an order or not.

Much more important is what Mr. Putin will do now. Sound advice from the White House should be accompanied by a totally unambiguous warning of an outcome that all would find profoundly regrettable. That is, if the Kremlin shields the murderers of journalist Anna Politkovskaya and ex-KGB spy Alexander Litvinenko, and if its propaganda continues to accuse "Western intelligence agencies" of those crimes, as it does at present, as it accused and continues to accuse the United States of sinking the submarine Kursk and of being behind the massacre of children in Beslan, then relations between the United States and Russia will be totally soured and will remain so until the last day of Mr. Putin's occupancy of the Kremlin.

Does Moscow Want a Nuclear Iran?

First published on April 9th, 2007

The recent scandal over the lack of payment by Iran to Russia for construction of the atomic power station at Bushehr has produced a wealth of commentaries in the Western media about a supposed change in Moscow's stance on Tehran's nuclear aspirations, bringing it closer to the American and European positions.

Thus, *The New York Times* reported that Russian officials had told Iran no fuel would be delivered if enrichment continued.

Before the printer's ink was dry on this assertion the minister of foreign affairs of the Russian Federation, Sergey Lavrov, had branded it blatant disinformation intended to cast a shadow over the traditionally friendly relations between Russia and Iran. The conflict over payment did indeed result more from problems over the kickbacks that accompany practically every major Russo-Iranian deal.

Evidently some top Russian official had not received his cut. Mr. Lavrov's indignation over *The New York Times'* report was entirely sincere, if rather naive. It is further confirmation that Moscow is happy to watch Iran continue toward acquiring nuclear weapons. For Moscow the best-case scenario for an end to the Iranian nuclear crisis would be an Israeli and/or American preventive strike against Iran's nuclear sites. This is because an Iranian nuclear bomb is something Russian leaders do not need. Iran is, after all, the only state in the world with official territorial claims against Russia. (Part of the Caspian seabed is disputed). Moreover, all the indignation of the Islamic world would be directed against Israel and the United States, which would also suit Moscow quite well.

Finally, Iran would doubtless retaliate by destroying the Saudi oil platforms and blocking the Straits of Hormuz, interrupting the export of oil from the Middle East for a while. The chekist oil barons who form the core of Vladimir Putin's entourage are already rubbing their hands in anticipation of this course of events. The ten or fifteen individuals who rule Russia, those in the current Politburo, also own Russia through their direct or indirect control of most of the country's oil and gas companies. How high might the price of a barrel of oil go? Two hundred dollars, three hundred dollars? Too much in their life—the regime's stability, their role on the world stage, and, finally, their personal wealth—depends on the number of dollars for a barrel of oil. They will not be repeating the Soviet leaders' mistake of passively watching the price of oil fall. They have, after all, plenty of scope for influencing the situation in the Middle East.

Every step of Moscow's Iranian policy in recent years has been aimed at moving events in this direction. By blocking or completely watering down UN Security Council resolutions on Iran, Moscow has facilitated Iran's nuclear program. By supplying Iran with TOR M-2 missile installations and negotiating over possible delivery of the more cutting-edge S-300 complex, Russia is effectively pushing Israel towards having to undertake a military solution of the problem. After the Russian antiaircraft installations to protect Iran's nuclear sites are fully commissioned, a military strike by Israel will no longer be feasible; but the alternative to a preventive strike is to see nuclear weapons and their means of delivery placed in the hands of some-one who believes in the need for a Final Solution of the Jewish Problem as profoundly and passionately as the late chancellor of Germany, Adolf Hitler. This is totally unacceptable to the Jewish state and, if Iran does not halt its nuclear program, a preventive strike is highly probable.

There are moderates in the Iranian leadership prepared to negotiate about discontinuing the industrial enrichment of uranium in return for a guarantee of international deliveries of nuclear fuel, but the recent spat with Russia over payment for the construction of Bushehr has greatly undermined their position. Moscow in any case made no demand that enrichment of uranium should be halted before deliveries of fuel were resumed. That would have been constructive and would have strengthened the hand of the moderates. Foreign Minister Lavrov, however, indignantly rejected any such approach and insisted that the problem was purely a misunderstanding about payment. Iran paid up, deliveries are being restarted, and the conclusion drawn from the incident by the Iranian establishment is wholly in favor of continuing with its nuclear project. The influential newspaper, *Resalat*, commented, "Russia's behavior is the best reason why Iran must insist on enriching uranium and producing nuclear fuel itself. You can't spend billions of dollars (on building a power plant) and then have to beg others for fuel."

As regards the motivation behind Russia's behavior in this financial dispute, the Iranian side understands that well and commented derisively. When the head of the Russian Federal Atomic Agency, Sergey Kirienko, complained that "since the middle of January we have not received a single kopek," his Iranian counterpart Mr. Saadi replied sarcastically, "It is true. We have never paid Mr. Kirienko a single kopek. Or a ruble either. For the past fifteen years we have been paying the Russians in dollars."

The nuances of how the Russian capitalist ministers behave may change, but their strategic aim remains unchanged: Moscow has consistently been the political, and now also the military, umbrella for the mullahs who are rushing to get their hands on nuclear weapons. The Kremlin fully understands that this will inevitably lead to military conflict. The war in Iraq has brought the Putin regime handsome political and economic dividends. Moscow is hoping that the feast will continue.

Russia's Western Neurosis

First published on February 26th, 2007

The attitude of the Russian political class to Europe, and to the West in general, over the last three to four centuries has always been contradictory, hypersensitive, and extremely emotional. The best Russian political text on the subject remains even today Alexander Blok's 1918 poem, "Scythians," with its famous lines about Russia: "She stares, she stares at you with hatred and with love" and "We will turn our Asiatic snout towards you."

Just as 300 years ago, and 200, and 20, we know perfectly well that we cannot do without Western technology and investments, and that autarky and an Iron Curtain spell economic and geopolitical disaster for Russia. We understand that Russian culture is an integral part of European culture.

And yet, the West seems to irritate us by the very fact of its existence. We see it as a psychological, informational and spiritual challenge. We are constantly trying to convince ourselves that the West is inherently hostile and malevolent toward Russia, because this flatters our vanity and helps to excuse our shortcomings and failures.

If you take any mainstream Russian publication and read the last one hundred articles dealing with foreign policy matters, ninety-eight will be full of bitterness, complaints, irritation, poison and hostility toward the West. This despite the fact that most of the authors of those articles like to spend as much time as possible in Western capitals and Western resorts, keep their money in Western banks, and send their children to study in Western schools and universities.

As in the famous poem a passionate declaration of love for Europe turns, at the slightest doubt as to whether it is reciprocated, into a threatening, "And if you won't, there's nothing we can lose, and we can answer you with treachery!"

What have "5,000 bayonets deployed in Bulgaria," three airplanes in Lithuania, Kosovo, or the Jew-baiter of Iran to do with anything? The whole lot of them are mere opportunities for the manic-depressive Russian elite to check and re-check its endless love-hate relationship with the West. That existential Russian question, "But do you respect me?" is in reality addressed, not to our latest drinking partner, but to the starry firmament in the West.

Several weeks ago, that question was asked again at the Munich Conference on Security Policy in the latest spiritual striptease show put on by the latest Russian Patient. It doesn't matter what his name is: Ivanov, Petrov, Sidorov, Yeltsin, Primakov, Putin.

For some reason it is considered statesmanlike and patriotic to pout your lips and enumerate before various Western audiences the same old list of "grievances" about the unipolar world, the ABM treaty, the expansion of NATO, the creeping up of NATO, our encirclement by NATO.

Wake up, intellectual "heavyweights" of Russia. What world and what century are you living in?

Where now is that mammoth, aggressive military machine of NATO you have so long been warning of? It truly has lumbered up to the sacred borders of the former Soviet Union, but not from the direction you expected. Indeed, my fear is that there it will meet its end, defending those borders from the advance of Islamic radicals. When NATO finally departs from Afghanistan and from history, the front of the Islamic revolution will cut through the countries of Central Asia. If we look a little further to the East, there too significant events are taking place.

"In September 2006 the Chinese People's Liberation Army conducted a ten-day military training exercise on an unprecedented scale in the Shenyang and Beijing Military Regions, the two most powerful of the seven Chinese MRs. These border Russia, Shenyang confronting the Far East Military Region and Beijing the Siberian Military Region of the armed forces of the Russian Federation. In the course of the exercise, units of the Shenyang MR performed a 1,000-kilometer advance into the territory of the Beijing MR and engaged in a training battle with units of that Region," said a February 12 article, "Greetings from China," in Izvestiya. "The nature of the exercise tells us that it is in preparation for war with Russia and, moreover, that what is being planned is not defense but attack. Against Taiwan this scenario makes no sense. Deep invasive operations are being worked out on dry land, in a region of steppes and mountains. The lie of the land in the region where the exercises were held is similar to that of the Trans-Baikal region, and 1,000 kilometers is precisely the distance from the Russo-Chinese border along the river Argun to Baikal."

But who is bothered about all this in our little psychiatric hospital? It is far more fun to go on about the usual grievances: bayonets in Bulgaria,

Russophobes in Courchevel, and slanderers of Russia in Scotland Yard. So, there we have it. In the not-too-distant future the centuries-old, tortuous psychological relationship between this patient and the West may finally be much simplified. No longer will anybody need to attend psychoanalytical conferences in Munich or turn their special Asiatic snout towards anyone there. Russia's Asiatic streak will be only too clear for all to see.

From Yeltsin to Putin

First published on April 23rd, 2007

The nature of the socio-economic system that has evolved in Russia since the late Boris Yeltsin came to power in the early 1990s is not a matter of dispute. All observers, from communist leader Gennadii Zuganov to Anatoly Chubais in Russia and from George Soros to Lawrence Summers in the US, described it in much the same terms: crony capitalism, family capitalism, oligarchic capitalism, gangster capitalism.

The choice of epithet is a matter of linguistic taste. It doesn't deny the reality of a system in which personal wealth and power are totally enmeshed, and where the word "corruption" is an inadequate description of what is going on. Classic corruption requires two parties: a businessman and a government official whom the businessman bribes. Russian oligarchs like Vladimir Potanin, Boris Berezovsky or Roman Abramovich didn't need to waste their time and money on government officials. They have themselves become either the top players in the state, or shadowy eminences in the entourage of the president with administrative state functions. Boris Berezovsky thundered on about this quite frankly in a famous interview in the Financial Times in October 1996. A shameless copulation of government power and private wealth was taken to its logical conclusion.

The system, which achieved its final form after the 1996 presidential elections, horrified even some of its creators by proving unexpectedly resistant to attempts to "de-privatize the state." One such creator was Anatoly Chubais. After parting company with the government, he said in an interview, "In 1996, I had to choose between a return to power of the communists and gangster capitalism. I chose gangster capitalism." Like many of the reformers, Chubais imagined that the main thing was not how to distribute property, but just to create property owners. The latter, having gotten thieving out of their system, would then set about increasing productivity. It didn't happen. What did happen was less a privatization of property than privatization of financial flows and primarily of budgetary revenues. It was a system that precluded the emergence of efficient property owners.

The reformers created a Frankenstein's monster that, having acquired a taste for fabulous self-enrichment, is now addicted to it and will never come off the needle of budgetary cash.

The reliably privatized Boris Yeltsin could not stand for election for a third time, for a number of constitutional and physiological reasons. In any case, the approach used in the 1996 campaign of scaring people with the communist threat was no longer effective. A fresh new idea was called for, and the intellectual menials duly came up with it.

The widespread mood of public disillusionment, irritation over failures, humiliation both from their personal situation and from Russia's obvious decline on the world stage might be expected to work against the party in power. The ploy of the regime's spin doctors was to harness this collective frustration to their own advantage. An enemy was identified, a straightforward method for reviving Russia suggested, and patriotism was misappropriated and privatized.

Even the most fanatical supporters of continuing the slaughter in Chechnya admitted that it was a war for the Kremlin, not for the Caucasus, and that the main problem it addressed was enabling power to be inherited by the Yeltsin "family's" favored successor.

Where would presidential hopeful Vladimir Putin and his popularity rating stand if it were not for the war in Chechnya? And where would popular support for the war, and with it, for the appointed successor, be but for the mysterious explosions that destroyed apartment blocks in Moscow just when the state authorities needed to whip up anti-Chechen hysteria.

It was naive to expect that Putin would make any attempt to dismantle the system of crony capitalism, when the iconic figures of that system are the prime movers behind the Putin project.

Putin's economic views are extremely vague, but he talks ceaselessly and very emotionally about the need to strengthen the role of the state. As someone who has spent his entire life working for police of one sort or another, he evidently does sincerely believe that this is a panacea for all economic ills. This is fundamentally erroneous, and given that the state has already been taken over by those with wealth and power, enhancing the role of the state will be catastrophic.

But enough of Putin. Ultimately, he is a replaceable figure. If there were no Putin, they would find a Poopkin. And they will find him in 2008. What matters is Putinism, a tool kit to enable the authorities to keep themselves in power.

Putinism is the highest and final stage of gangster capitalism in Russia, the stage at which the bourgeoisie throws overboard the banner of democratic freedoms and human rights.

Putinism is a war, a rallying of the nation based on hatred of a particular ethnic group. It is an attack on freedom of speech, a dumbing down of the population by the media. It is isolation from the outside world, portraying the West and the US in particular as an eternal enemy of Russia. It is the continuing degradation of the petro-economy under the guise of pseudo-growth due to exorbitant oil prices.

Putinism is (to use a favorite expression of our current president) a "control shot" in the head of Russia.

It is the inheritance bequeathed to us by Boris Yeltsin.

Lugovoi for President

First published on July 30th, 2007

In the latest interview given by Andrei Lugovoy, whose extradition on the suspicion of having murdered ex-KGB agent Alexander Litvinenko is being sought by Great Britain, there was a remarkable moment, which seems not to have been fully appreciated. Lugovoy, still rather diffidently but already with unmistakable pride, mentioned that when he is seen in public he usually finds himself surrounded by people who want to shake his hand, congratulate him on his valor, and ask for his autograph.

"Well, haven't you thought about a career in politics?" the interviewer asked. It is a pity they did not pursue this topic, which certainly merits further exploration.

Let us start by looking at what Lugovoy told us. Perhaps surprisingly, he seems not to have wondered why he should be enjoying such an enthusiastic reception from his compatriots and why they were so eager to acquire his autograph. Were they showing solidarity with a victim unjustly hounded by the British Crown Prosecution Service? Come off it! When did Russians ever ask victims for their autographs? I have myself exciting the interest of the Russian Public Prosecutor's Office for several months now, and have yet to encounter a single autograph-hunter.

In Russia you get asked for your autograph if you have made it, if you are a proper hero: an ice-hockey player, a cosmonaut, a high-society prostitute, or an executioner.

The list of unspeakable crimes allegedly committed in the course of his brief life by the late Alexander Litvinenko grows longer with every day that passes, and is such that any right-minded Russian patriot could only thirst to see the traitor subjected to the supreme measure of national retribution. Only one such patriot, however, was granted the great honor of being allowed to perform this act, and that is why Lugovoy is being asked for his autograph.

This should not, of course, be taken to mean that the patriots so enthused by Lugovoy's stupendous achievement concede the justice of the allegations of the British investigation. The social awareness of homo putinicus, meticulously burnished by the television propagandists, is such that pride in the achievement of this spook and indignation at the infamous campaign unleashed against him by the calumniators of Russia can jangle in harmony within his breast without the slightest suggestion of self-contradiction, and indeed bring out vivid new hues in each other.

We are evidently facing the mystery of that holistic quality of Russians' synthetic thinking which has proved so unfathomable to those of other nations, so unyielding to every analytical scalpel, and about which our Slavophiles and Eurasians wrote at such length.

But to return to the interviewer's question: is this not the ideal solution to the problem of Putin's heir, which is threatening to divide the nation's elite? If we compare these two potential presidential candidates, Lugovoy in 2007 and Putin in 1999, we can only be struck by a number of obvious coincidences: the same modest social background, the same KGB alma mater, the same criminal vocabulary, the same mentality and physique, and the same mercilessness towards "enemies of the people."

The underworld manners of both go hand in hand with that lively interest in business so essential if "liberal reforms" are to be continued in Russia. Finally, there is the additional, highly significant coincidence that both of them, at the start of their political careers, were largely indebted, perhaps even totally indebted, to the oligarch Boris Berezovsky but subsequently fell out with him.

As regards the actual achievements of the candidates in their basic professional activity, Lugovoy in 2007 seems to have the edge. To succeed in carrying out a large-scale operation in the middle of London beats doing a desk job in the GDR-USSR House of Friendship in Dresden.

So why should we suppose that the Russian people would not take to their hearts this executioner with the rank of lieutenant colonel, just as eight years ago they took to their hearts another lieutenant colonel with the nickname of Stasi? Would the sybaritic, globe-trotting Lugovoy agree to wear the crown of Monomakh? We have all seen Putin's face change over the course of the last eight years.

Actually, Lugovoy's face has also changed markedly during the last eight months of press conferences.

Two living portraits of Dorian Gray.

Two faces of the new Russia that is "rising from its knees."

Why Russia's Youth Hate America

First published on August 28th, 2007

"Well, you hang negroes in America!" This was the clinching argument in any ideological dispute between the lady administrator of the Soviet Intourist travel agency and American tourists who had been kept awake all night by bedbugs.

Since then much has changed. Russia's Liberal Revolution, long anticipated by generations of Westernizers, finally occurred and bedbugs were liquidated as a class, at least in five-star hotels in the metropolis. There have long been no lynchings of blacks in America either. Instead they, along with Armenians, Tatars, and Tadjiks, are murdered by the dozen every year in Russia by the grandchildren of those same lady administrators and for no other reason than that they are Africans, Armenians, Tatars, or Tadjiks.

Their grandmothers and grandfathers clearly didn't give a damn about the fate of those "negroes they hang in America" if they brought up their grandchildren this way.

I imagine, indeed I can see from the expression on his face, that our Foreign Minister, Mr. Sergey Lavrov, is simply longing to silence the elegant lady talking to him by using that same killer argument when she starts really getting to him with her sententious comments on the fate of democracy in Russia. Then, however, he looks more closely at Condoleeza Rice and stops himself just in time. He needs fresh, up-to-date ideological arguments. He has found them. Indeed, they have been handed to him on a plate.

Sarah Mendelson and Theodore Gerber published an article, "Young Russia's Enemy No. 1," in the August 3rd edition of the Washington Post about a public opinion research project they conducted in Russia jointly with the Levada Analytic Center. They surveyed 1,802 young people aged between eighteen and twenty-nine, and discovered a considerable increase in hostility toward the United States. This is hardly surprising after an almost three-year campaign of ceaseless, hysterical anti-Americanism, initiated by Vladimir Putin's famous post-Beslan address to the nation in which he announced that "behind the Islamic terrorists there stand more powerful and more dangerous, traditional enemies of Russia."

Ms. Mendelson and Mr. Gerber are fully aware of the machinery of this state-sponsored brainwashing, but comment also that "human rights violations associated with US counterterrorism policies have played a role."

They discovered, for example, that 52 percent of those surveyed believe the United States "tortures terrorism suspects," up to 57 percent condemn such practices, and that this largely determines their hostility toward the United States.

I wholly share the passion with which these worthy researchers condemn the violations of human rights that have indeed taken place in the Abu Ghraib and Guantanamo Bay prisons. I could only be heartened to find that 57 percent of my young compatriots are as irreconcilable towards such intolerable practices as are the intellectuals of Europe and America. One thing, however, disconcerts me.

These young people live in Russia and they know very well that, whatever the propagandists say, Abu Ghraib and Guantanamo Bay, despite all the abominations practiced there, are a holiday resort by comparison not only with the notorious interrogation center in the village of Chernokozovo but with any ordinary Russian prison camp or any ordinary Russian barracks. To date the Americans have not beaten up their Islamist prisoners to the extent of Private Andrei Sychev, who had to have his legs and genitals amputated in hospital.

Fifty-four percent of those surveyed, practically the same number of people, consider that Josef Stalin "did more good than bad" for Russia. This is not a historical but a moral judgement on the part of our young "human rights champions." Our young patriots believe there are causes so noble that they can and should be furthered by the slaughter of millions of Russian people.

The "captives of Abu Ghraib and Guantanamo Bay" are just the same cynical propaganda currency as those hanged blacks were for Intourist's housekeeper. As it happens, a couple of prisoners freed by the Americans under the pressure of progressive world opinion have already been tortured in Russian interrogation cells.

Russia's youth hate America not because of its treatment of the prisoners of Guantanamo, about whom our young patriots really do not care. Our young people hate America because that is what the "grown-ups" are telling them to do twenty-four hours a day on television. Our secret-policemen-turned-capitalists who commission this music hate America twice over.

Firstly, because that is their job. These fathers of the nation have no ideology other than anti-Americanism to get the masses to rally round their unabashed thievery, which is unprecedented in the history even of Russia.

In the second place, they hate America from the bottom of their hearts. They let the cat out of the bag last year in the infamous Evstafiev-Falin report on threats to Russian national security. As threat No. 1, they blazoned the risk of blackmail of Russian officials who maintain bank accounts abroad. They have stored up their riches not in heaven and they keep their treasure chests not in countries so socially akin to us as North Korea, Iran or Venezuela, but in those same damnable United States, and hate them all the more because they fear being exposed. You are quite right, Ms. Mendelson and Mr. Gerber, Abu Ghraib and Guantanamo Bay really should be shut down. But you are wrong if you think that will make America any less hated in Russia. It is not Abu Ghraib we hate you for.

We, or rather our "elite," which incites this hatred, hates you because it loathes itself. And that is a very long-term problem.

A Missed Opportunity. (Our Niche)

First published on October 15th, 2007

The time when Russia and the US viewed each other as ene-mies or as a strategic threat has come to an end. Russia and the US are currently engaged as partners and friends, responding jointly to the new challenges of the 21st century. Our nations are allies in the global war on terror. The pursuit of a trust-based partnership between Russia and the US remains one of the top priorities of Russian foreign policy. Russia and the US both agree on what constitutes a threat to international secu-rity. It's not a global nuclear disaster or military posturing by the US or NATO that pose a threat to Russia. The threat lies hidden in the Caucasus and Asian borderlands.

Just which Judeomason, NATO supporter, or Internet traitor put pen to paper to write these words?! What danger could possibly lie hidden in the Asian borderlands when we just hugged it out with our Chinese bros in the Ural Mountains during joint military maneuvers, the first time Chinese troops were there since Genghis Khan approached from the banks of the Yangtze? The two nations are now together. And which international terror-ists are we talking about?

Perhaps it's those illustrious leaders of the world's liberation move-ments—people like Mashal, Nasralla, or maybe Ahmadinejad, the president of our friendly neighbor Iran who understandably pointed out that although there was no Holocaust it might be a good idea to start one?

I won't keep you in suspense any longer, my patriotic reader. The words that have caused so much offense and outrage belong to Vladimir Vladimirovich Putin. The first two sentences come from a signed joint state-ment Putin and George Bush issued at the May 23rd 2002 Moscow Summit.

The rest is a quote from Putin's speech at his meeting with MFA employees several days later.

Putin was totally correct. He knew exactly what he was talking about. Six months earlier, for the first time in Russian military history, Putin had successfully resolved the country's security issues (on the Afghanistan border) without losing a single Russian soldier. Acting against the advice of those closest to him and of the Russian foreign policy establishment, the president simply made other people (the Americans) do all the work for him. Russia realized in real terms that having the US as an ally would help solve the country's security woes, This new piece of knowledge could have drastically altered the geopolitical mindset of the Russian political class. Putin understood this earlier and better than most in his circle; he clearly saw the potential opportunities these new realities had to offer including in the Far East region.

Not for nothing have I always referred to the man as "the most outstanding mediocrity of the Russian political class." But then came hordes of Lavrovs, Primakovs, Patrushevs, and their ilk and little by little they were able to bring Putin down to their level of thinking. Five years have passed and the official Moscow line has started to sound quite a bit different: "The differences of opinion we have with the United States are so fundamental that a position of constructive ambiguity is hardly appropriate. Russia cannot afford to sit on the sidelines in the global conflict of civilizations being waged."

The political strategist Gleb Pavlovsky, closely aligned with the Kremlin, presented recently a new Russian foreign policy vision concept. It turns out that Russian foreign policy has a "global mission" assigned by all of progressive humanity—to contain the United States.

"Putin has found himself a unique niche and has plunged right in." What a powerful hypersexualized metaphor! The father of the nation, plunging into a niche.

This "unique," anti-American niche, as it were, is teeming with paranoid dictators of all stripes.

Russia's Kleptocracy

First published on November 2nd, 2007

The corporatist kleptocracy being erected by Russian President Vladimir Putin is profoundly misunderstood. Liberal defenders and apologists of the Putin regime, from Dmitry Trenin in Russia to President George W. Bush (who recently looked deeply this time not into Putin's soul but into the soul of the Russian people and discovered there is "a kind of basic Russian DNA which is a centralized authority"), trot out a pet argument which migrates from one publication to another. It goes something like this: What is most important for Russia right now is not abstract "democracy" but the development of capitalism. A growing middle class of property owners with a vested interest in security for their property will ultimately demand the establishment of liberal institutions. There is nothing fundamentally new or specific about this. Any freedom, as the history of the world testifies, begins with freedom for the barons and gradually extends down, to finally include the ordinary Joe on the street.

So, a middle class of property owners in Russia will come with time, we are to believe, and they will recognize the importance of property rights and introduce liberal institutions in Russia. This extremely popular theory totally ignores the actual nature of Russian capitalism. The right to property in Russia is entirely conditional on the property owner's loyalty to the Russian government. The system is tending to evolve, not in the direction of freedom and a post-industrial society, but rather back toward feudalism, when the sovereign distributed privileges and lands to his vassals and could take them away at any moment. The only difference is that, in today's Russia, what Putin is distributing and taking away is not lands but gas and oil companies.

Over the last ten to fifteen years, a mutant has evolved which is neither socialism nor capitalism but some hitherto unknown creature. Its defining characteristics are a merging of money and power, the institutionalization of corruption, and domination of the economy by major corporations, chiefly trading in commodities, which flourish at the expense of the administrative resources they have privatized.

The Kremlin Dreamers

First published on July 10th, 2008

The "Kremlin Thaw" faction is, in my view, doomed to defeat (and, needless to say, this will be a defeat for Russia as a whole), because its philosophy, rhetoric, and actions are fatally self-contradictory.

Ot-tepel', the Russian word for "thaw," suggests a moving away, a negation, a rejection, a condemnation of something previously existing, a stigmatizing of it as, if not downright harmful, then certainly less than perfect and in need of revision.

The writer Ilya Ehrenburg had good reason to put this libertarian word into circulation not in 1952, before the death of Stalin, but in 1954 when what needed revision was safely entombed in the mausoleum and not puffing its pipe in the presidium. Ehrenburg waited until a time when Stalin's successor could remark with studied casualness, "That outstanding figure in the world Communist movement, the permanent leader of the Party and Government, Joseph Vissarionovich Stalin, did, unfortunately, commit a number of serious theoretical errors in the last years of his life, in particular in his work, *Economic Problems of Socialism*."

But what are you to do, esteemed reformers, if the "outstanding figure" is still leading both the Party and the Government? Against whom and against what is your Thaw a reaction? Two competing answers have been suggested by the ideologists of the new Thaw. The first is borrowed from the ideological heritage of the Thaw of half a century ago: "Dark forces surround the ruler."

"Serious errors, and on occasions even acts of villainy, were committed by the criminal Beria-Abamukov gang of adventurers who placed themselves above the Party and wormed their way into the confidence of Joseph Vissarionovich in the latter years of his life." One could, of course, simply re-use this artless framework, inserting the names of today's Chekist secret policemen, but it was much less dangerous in those bygone days to blame everything on Lavrenty Beria and Viktor Abakumov after they had been shot. Before then they might have objected very effectively . Evidently aware of the inherent shakiness of such a construct while all the Abakumovs are still alive, the Thaw faction has recently proposed an alternative myth.

There were no "errors," let alone acts of villainy, in the preceding period; and no dark forces.

It was the fault of the times, difficult times, the first phase of modernization. In this first phase, indeed, democratization is not essential and authoritarianism, a limitation of pluralism as in South Korea, for example, is to be preferred. In the new phase, however, which happily coincides with the inauguration of a new president, the suggestion is that there should be "top-down" liberalization of Russia's political life.

It is a neat idea with only one shortcoming. The reference to South Korea would have been better left out. It may not go down well with the rulers. Where, we have to ask, did two South Korean presidents in office during that "first phase of modernization" end their political careers? That's right, in prison. In fact the directors of the chebols, the state corporations whose non-viability became apparent during the 1998 crisis, are also, for the most part, in prison. And what is it that the veteran of the Dresden KGB residency Vladimir Putin's buddy Sergei Chemezov, is currently engaged in? That's right, he is building the biggest chaebol in the world.

The comparison with South Korea and other Southeast Asian tiger economies is false, and misleading. In the 1980s and early 1990s, those countries were effecting a transition from an agrarian to an industrial society. This phase of modernization by Stalinist, hyper-authoritarian, barbaric methods is something Russia had already endured in the 1930s–1950s. As the 21st century began, the task it faced was quite different: the breakthrough to a post-industrial economy. If this were something that could be achieved by digging more foundation pits and canals, Putin and his thieving Chekists would be invaluable.

But it is a task that simply cannot be accomplished using authoritarian methods. The knowledge economy is an economy of free people, a category of society which, as a recent survey by the Levada Centre revealed, has every intention of emigrating from Putin's Russia. In South Korea the authoritarian model of development was completely played out by the mid-1990s, and the past decade has seen fundamental economic and political shifts there.

Accordingly, there is no way anyone can describe the years 2001-2007 in Russia as a first, inevitable, authoritarian phase of modernization. It was the highest and final phase of gangster-bureaucratic capitalism. Total control of the electoral process, the media, and the judicial system was something the ruling clique needed, not to accomplish civilized tasks that a backward people supposedly was not yet capable of understanding. It was needed purely for the purpose of concealing their thievery, which was unbridled and unprecedented even in the history of Russia.

These truths are well known to the academics in all manner of Institutes of Modern Development and Centers of Political Technologies who write scholarly papers about top-down liberalization, as well as to the people who commission their studies. The trouble is that, as they seek to spread enlightenment, the academics are organically incapable of shaking off old habits of respectfully kissing the ass of the state authorities. They cannot do so because they are umbilically tied, both socially and financially, to the regime. They are a component part of it.

The constructive copulation with the state authorities strikes them as a cunning way of gradually injecting liberal values. But the regime will not need even to snap its fingers at them to get them to abandon this futile aspiration. Here, more or less, is what will happen:

Our collective Beria-Abakumovs will tomorrow blow something up in the Caucasus. Actually, why tomorrow, when something is already being blown up there every day? The moment a serious crisis arises, these so-called liberals will forget all about their Thaw and push each other aside in the scramble to get to the microphones and be the first to yell, "The Russian army is being reborn in the Kodor Gorge/Gali District, and anybody who thinks otherwise is a traitor."

The "Grad"s of August

First published on August 12th, 2008

On that first worrying day of the War, from beyond the Himalayas, indeed from China itself, a voice spoke to mankind and set everything in its moral context. It was the ineffably pure voice of Vladimir Putin, last of the Mahatmas, who, as he has told us himself, has had nobody to talk to since the death of Gandhi.

"What is happening in South Ossetia is barbaric aggression. They are using "Grad" (Hail) missiles. These are not a precisely targeted weapon but a means of indiscriminate carpet bombardment."

The use of "Grad" batteries by the Russian army to systematically bombard Chechen towns and villages, killing Chechen and Russian civilians, is a fact well known and confirmed by numerous documents and eyewitness accounts.

These war crimes by Russian troops were not condemned but praised to the skies by official propaganda and The Best Masters of Culture who are favorites of our redoubtable President.

Indeed, on more than one occasion the Mahatma himself has been observed sitting in a front row warmly applauding the soul-searing rendition of that patriotic hit which has become something of an anthem of the Second Chechen War: "On the battlefield we have the Grad, And behind us Putin and Stalingrad."

Now, however, we are told that the use of Grad batteries is barbaric, indiscriminate carpet bombing, which makes the appropriate reference not to Stalingrad but to The Hague. Putin's denunciation of the use of "Grad" missiles sounds like a prior admission of guilt.

The only people with any moral right to condemn Mikheil Saakashvili for the assault on Tskhinvali are those who condemned Russia's leaders for their methods of "re-establishing constitutional order" in Chechnya, and for an assault on Grozny which turned it into a second Dresden.

In 1999 and the following years, just as in 1968, only isolated individuals spoke out against the general fervor over a "renaissance of the Russian army in Chechnya" and they, needless to say, were promptly stigmatized as traitors.

Whatever reasons may have prompted the Georgian leaders to attempt to resolve the problems of South Ossetia by force (a desire to restore territorial integrity, the shelling by separatists of Georgian positions and Georgian villages, the hope that Russia would not intervene, etc.), they do not justify the use of force, let alone the firing of volleys of missiles into Tskhinvali. Attempting to resolve issues of territorial unity by force inevitably lead to loss of life.

Be that as it may, the bombing of Gori, Poti, the sea blockade, and the sinking of Georgian vessels by Russia have nothing to do with "peacekeeping" or "defending the civilian population of South Ossetia." This is aggression and military (not "humanitarian") intervention, accompanied by cynical lying by Russian officials.

The killing of civilians in Chechnya was criminal, the killing of civilians in Tskhinvali was criminal, and it is criminal for Russia to be killing civilians today in Gori and Poti.

Our Nation's Leader is in great form again. Gone is that slightly depressed and disconcerted look during the inauguration of his "heir" and for some time after it. In the element of war he is like a fish in water. His pronouncements are delivered with elan, panache. He is manifestly enjoying himself, flexing his facial muscles. He is convincing. There is a lot of truth in what he is saying about the killing of civilians in Tskhinvali and that, after all that has happened, it may be impossible for the Georgians and Ossetians to be reconciled. Nobody raises, or is likely in the near future to raise, such other issues as the tens of thousands of civilians killed in Chechnya, or those who are currently being killed in raids on Georgian cities.

Now, however, as salvoes of "Grad"s are fired and bombs are dropped, a problem which has been disturbing him and the whole Russian "political elite" for so long, that problem of his third (and in reality, life-long) presidential term, has been magically resolved. Where is President Medvedev today? What does he amount to anyway? He is a minor official whom the Nation's Leader publicly, in front of the television cameras, lectures on how Russia's supposed "head of state" should act: "and, I think it will be best, Dmitriy Anatolievich, if you advise the Military Prosecutor's Office. . . . I repeat, it would be best if the Military Prosecutor's Office were given the requisite instruction from the President." At great length and with evident satisfaction, the Prime Minister delivers his views on foreign policy and military topics, matters which from a formal viewpoint are completely outside his competence.

The Gatherer of the Lands of Russia, irrespective of the post he formally occupies, clearly has a mission paved with good intentions and extending many years ahead into the future. Who is going to try to obstruct it with quasi-constitutional quibbles about terms in office? In domestic policy terms, this is the main outcome of his "Second Victorious Little War," and that, evidently, was its main aim.

A Sorry Excuse for a Fuhrer and a Sorry Excuse for an Empire

First published on December 18th, 2014

Two communist empires came to an end in 1991. The world first witnessed the collapse of Yugoslavia, an event swiftly followed by the implosion of the Soviet regime. The causes leading to these collapses were identical but the actual processes were not. The "spiritual bonds" of communism disintegrated completely and nothing remained to keep the younger brother, Serbia, in the orbit of his older sibling, Russia. The nature of each empire's demise was largely dictated by the Serbian and Russian people themselves and their particular view of what was occurring. If we take a closer look at the charismatic leaders of that period—Milosevic in Serbia and Yeltsin in Russia—we see that both were dyed-in-the-wool populists. The vast majority of voters supported them and their policies.

The Serbs, utterly spellbound, even obsessed, with the idea of a provincial empire and desperate to keep all of Yugoslavia for themselves, jumped at the chance to carve out a Greater Serbian World from the old Soviet borders. In the process, they started and then lost at least half a dozen wars, ultimately leading to the loss of tens of thousands of lives.

In Russia there was no lack of support for splitting up the Soviet empire in much the same way. The State Committee on the State of Emergency actually launched an *imperial* coup, not a communist one. One of the leaders of "victorious democracy," Yevgeny Popov, even called for the friendly dismemberment of Ukraine using the same border template that Putin is currently employing. But when it came time to ratify the Belovezha Accords, the documents that divided up the USSR using the official borders of the Soviet republics, only a handful of people showed up in Moscow to protest. The lunatic fringe in favor of empire, which these days would include Igor Girkin, everyone's favorite war criminal, headed to the Balkans as a consolation prize and immediately began murdering Croats and Bosnians en masse. What is interesting, however, is that back then Vladimir Putin was nowhere to be found. Our Chekist lieutenant colonel was kind of flying under the radar at those crucial moments in history and showing no signs of any designs on an empire.

During the short period when the Emergency Committee was seemingly in charge, Putin was seen walking obediently behind the mayor of St. Petersburg carrying his briefcase while his boss battled the coup plotters in Russia's second city. And once the "shining forces of democracy and progress" won their victory, Putin immersed himself in financial schemes such as "Colored metals and petroleum products in exchange for doughnut holes." These projects served as the first little bricks in the foundation of Putin's personal financial empire. In hindsight we can see that the Yeltsin reformers and the coup plotters were mostly in agreement on the strategies necessary to hand over state-run industries to the privileged classes. If Yanaev, Pavlov, and their ilk had gotten their way, could you really imagine them turning down the tasty morsels of state-owned property? They had already been eagerly stuffing their pockets, after all, with help from Chernomyrdin and Alekperov.

It seems all the Soviet apparatchiks had come to some kind of agreement in the corridors of the Lubyanka during Andropov's premiership. To be honest, that fire-breathing dragon of communism, so spectacularly vanquished on August 19-21, had drawn its last breath on its own by that time, especially in the hearts and minds of its main proponents. The leadership had begun swapping out portraits of Lenin for those of Benjamin Franklin. The disagreements these groups had were on a different matter entirely. The putsch supporters wanted the state-run industries, yes, but also the grandeur of empire thrown in for good measure. But Yeltsin, ever the pragmatist, understood that even a more modest empire was not in the cards, and that no amount of bloodshed could help matters. The stark lesson of Yugoslavia was there for all to see.

A classic parody of the Russian World depicts an elderly dictator and his mindless attempts to travel back twenty-three years in the past via time machine in order to replay the events surrounding the Soviet Union's collapse. He tries to play it out using the Yugoslav game plan, drawing out the agony of his moldy kleptocracy by powdering its nose with a Louis XIV-style ideocratic project along the lines of the fascism of Hitler or the communism of Stalin.

Although at the moment there are no politicians in the West on the scale of a Churchill or a Roosevelt, it seems the Chamberlains of the group are slowly coming around and finding an effective way to counter Moscow and its escalatory nuclear weapon sabre-rattling.

The Kremlin's nuclear weapon rhetoric is intended to undermine Article 5 of the NATO charter. The West has acknowledged it, analyzed it, and taken necessary steps, namely deploying, on a permanent basis, NATO military contingents to the Baltics and Poland. These contingents include American soldiers. The actual size of them is not that important. They are not there to engage in offensive combat activities and let's hope they won't have to engage in defensive ones either. The mere fact that American enlisted soldiers and officers are present is important. They act as a boots-on-the-ground containment strategy, hostages and suicide bombers all in one. For over a year now, the sabre-rattlers in the Kremlin, from Kiselyov and his "radioactive ash" comments to the incomparable Anna Semenovich and her "Don't Make my Iskanders Laugh" t-shirt, have counted on one thing: being able to deploy their little green men to the Baltics and have them rattle their nuclear nightsticks. Europe and the US would then be sent into a paralytic stupor as they pondered the question: "Are you willing to die for Narva?" But now, the largely symbolic presence of American troops in the vicinity of Narva changes things drastically from a psychological standpoint. If even one armed little man steps foot on Estonian soil, it would mean the Russian Federation has entered a full-scale war with the United States. And so we see the existential question turned back on Putin and his business-partners: "Esteemed experts in corruption, are you really willing to die for Narva?"

The Tolling of the Bells

First published on October 8th, 2017

> "President Kennedy died a soldier—in a hail of
> bullets."
> —Charles de Gaulle, President of France

In 2013, fifty years after the tragedy in Dallas, archival documents in the US pertaining to the assassination of John F. Kennedy had still not been fully made public. When the archives were opened this year, we got to see only a portion of them. Many documents remain classified due to "national security concerns."

After looking through the documents made public this week, my view of what took place that day in Dallas has not changed all that much; there are a few nuances to point out, however. First off I would like to articulate what I see to be a fundamental truth concerning Lee Harvey Oswald. It's something that has been ignored for fifty-four years by the vast majority of Americans, including so-called "Russia specialists," but is perfectly obvious to the millions of us living in the USSR at the time.

It's a story of a young, left-leaning American defecting to the USSR in 1959 for ideological reasons but then becoming disenchanted with the socialist paradise he finds there. He informs his ever-vigilant handlers that he intends to return to the US. By then it is 1962. It is a bit of a stretch, I'll admit, but I actually can see the honorable and compassionate gentlemen at the KGB accepting this slap in the face and not hesitating to issue all the required documentation for Oswald to return to the territory of the USSR's main adversary. Instead of, let's say, putting him in jail for a while for petty street crime or looking the other way as the guy crashes his car.

Remember, Stalin's repressive regime was long gone and we were deep into Khrushchev's thaw. Times were different, more open. When police opened fire on a labor demonstration in Novocherkassk that same year, only twenty-six people were killed and seven later sentenced to death.

What I will never believe is that the Soviet Union would allow Oswald's wife—Marina Prusakova—to leave her country of birth simply because her idiot husband had become disenchanted, if you can believe it, with the grand ideals of socialism. The relevant authorities had accepted this accomplished athlete, komsomol member, distance-course student, and shock worker as comrade Oswald's legal spouse. I would also say that no one living in the Soviet Union in 1962 will ever believe it.

The Oswalds could have left the Soviet Union without incident in only one capacity—as agents recruited by Soviet intelligence. My favorite of the documents just now declassified after more than 50 years is a dispatch from a CIA agent in Moscow dated December 4, 1963. This agent had been on the receiving end of leaks from a high-ranking "source" (sorry, the source furnished "reliable information"). To give the reader an idea of just how well American spies understood their "main adversary" at the time, I reproduce the text in its entirety:

> A source who has furnished reliable information in the past advised on Dec. 4, 1963 that the news of the assassination was greeted in the Kremlin by great shock and consternation and church bells tolled in the memory of President Kennedy.

Over the course of those fifty-four years, not a single expert at Langley was able to trace the origin of this "dispatch" to Stalin's famous resolution (issued for much better reasons) from June 17th, 1941: "Tell this source to f*ck off! It's not a source at all! It's disinformation!"

False expressions of religious feeling have been used for generations within Soviet intelligence; it's a classic technique. Our little major, Vladimir Putin, born in 1952, was no exception when he tried to recruit George W. Bush in 2001 with that touching story about risking his life in a fire to save a crucifix that had been blessed in the Holy Land. Two diplomats (one American, one Russian) who happened to be present at this session of Lubyanka-style mesmerism told me that Bush, looking deep into Putin's soul, even wept.

On the topic of bells tolling for the murdered President Kennedy, Americans have been weeping with heavy emotion for more than five decades over the loss. One other interesting document released recently is a detailed CIA account of a meeting that took place at the Soviet embassy in Mexico City on September 26, 1963 between Oswald and Valery Vladimirovich Kostikov from the 13th Directorate of the KGB. Kostikov was the head Soviet "wet worker" for the Western hemisphere and was working at the embassy in a consular cover position. At first, Kostikov met with Oswald in the presence of two other colleagues. After that they spoke alone for about twenty minutes.

A record of this meeting exists not because the CIA was following Oswald but because it was following Kostikov. This marked the first (!) time since Oswald's return from the USSR that he appeared on the CIA's radar. He then promptly disappeared from it. No information whatsoever concerning Oswald, so full of sorrow and grief, was ever passed on to the relevant agencies: to the Secret Service protecting Kennedy, for example, or to the FBI field office in Dallas in charge of security during the president's visit to Dallas.

President Kennedy was assassinated by an agent recruited by the Soviet Union. I completely disagree with the canonic assessments made by Russian historians in plain clothes that the Soviet leadership would have had no motive to murder Kennedy. There was a motive, and a serious one at that.

The way the Cuban Missile Crisis had played out (the success of the US's naval blockade, the removal of Soviet missiles from Cuba under UN supervision) made the Soviet Union look weak. I am certain that is how the Kremlin interpreted the entire ordeal. What was even more humiliating—it was the young American president who people first saw as weak after the Khrushchev-Kennedy summit in Vienna in 1961.

I can clearly remember the style and wording of Moscow propaganda right after the Cuban Missile Crisis. I was struck by how perplexed and self-conscious it seemed, something uncharacteristic and even inconceivable for Soviet agitprop at the time. With an air of detachment, the events were described as a compromise. What's more, the entire leadership, starting with Khrushchev and then copied by his stooges and half-wits, pronounced this unpleasant foreign word with the stress on the second syllable. This compromise was then somehow justified and explained away to the rest of the population. I remember one party presidium member giving an important speech, broadcast to the entire country (I believe it was the usual November 6th address), where the compromise was somehow justified by quoting Lenin in dialogue with his comrades telling them how necessary it was to sign the Treaty of Brest-Litovsk (!).

And I thought to myself, "Wow, if they are trying to pass off this compromise to us, their subjects, as a repeat of that sleazy Treaty of Brest-Litovsk, I wonder how the inner circle interprets it?"

It was at this very time that the upper levels of the nomenclature began to conspire against Khruschev. The plan was put into action two years later.

We can place the blame for this new Treaty of Brest-Litovsk squarely on Khrushchev and his failed escapade in Cuba, coupled with his hollow boasting about missiles that we launch as if they were little sausages.

According to the laws of a communist-era prison, a mob boss who has debased himself has lost his title. There can be no doubt that Soviet intelligence and the leadership in general believed that Kennedy had humiliated the Soviet Union and the Soviet system in the eyes of the entire world.

The assassination was aided by stunning negligence on the part of American intelligence. It was almost as if they wanted a crime to take place. All of this became clear, of course, to the Warren Commission and top American officials as they investigated. But the US government still believes it cannot officially acknowledge it.

How to Identify the Thieves in the Kremlin and their American Agents

First published on November 13th, 2017, with Anders Åslund, Daniel Fried, and Andrei Illarionov

On August 2, 2017, US President Donald J. Trump signed H. R. 3364, Countering America's Adversaries Through Sanctions Act (CAATSA), into law. Section 241 of the Act calls on "the Secretary of the Treasury, in consultation with the Director of National Intelligence and the Secretary of State" to submit to Congress a detailed report—with the option of making part of it classified—including "identification of the most significant senior foreign political figures and oligarchs in the Russian Federation, as determined by their closeness to the Russian regime and their net worth." Section 241 mandates that the report address the relationship of these persons to Russian President Vladimir Putin, and identify their corruption, estimated net worth, and known sources of income. The section also poses similar questions about Russian parastatal entities of diffuse ownership but serving the state. The Kremlin Report, as it might be termed, is due on or around February 1, 2018.

Section 241 has generated intense interest, even anxiety, within Moscow's political and business classes, more so than any other section of H. R. 3364. It is clear why. Speculation is abundant in Moscow about who among political figures, oligarchs, and others may be listed, and what that might mean for them, for Russia's ruling political and business elite in general, and for Russia's already beleaguered standing in the West.

These anxieties suggest that the Kremlin Report can serve US, Western, and genuine Russian interests in two ways:

First, it can signal to the current Russian political and business classes that, as individuals, their interests would best be served by maintaining a distance from the Putin regime. It also may indicate that these groups would be better off if the Russian leadership refrained from starting new aggressive wars or attacking the political system of the United States and other democratic countries, as it did during the 2016 US presidential campaign and subsequent elections throughout Europe.

Second, the Kremlin Report's identification of corrupt individuals close to the Putin regime may expose them to increased scrutiny and potential action by those US government institutions enforcing US laws and regulations beyond sanctions, such as measures against money laundering and other financial malfeasance, e.g., Treasury's Financial Action Task Force (FATF) and the Financial Crimes Enforcement Network (FinCEN), among others. That process could in turn lead to future actions to freeze the assets of corrupt individuals and, at the right point, legal processes to return ill-gotten assets to the Russian people.

Metrics for Identifying Senior Political Figures, Oligarchs, and Parastatal Entities Close to the Kremlin senior political figures, oligarchs, and parastatal entities constitute what we may call members of the Russian ruling elite. Section 241 stipulates several metrics to be used in identifying them. We note two:

- Closeness of senior political figures, business people, or parastatal entities to the Russian political regime. This could be measured a number of ways, including involvement (open or hidden) in the Putin regime's aggressive (or even illegal) actions. Such actions include Russia's interference in the 2016 US presidential election, as well as its military aggression against Georgia and Ukraine, including the purported annexation of Crimea; responsibility for bombing civilians in Chechnya and Syria; and murders of Yuriy Shchekochikhin, Anna Politkovskaya, Alexander Litvinenko, Sergei Magnitsky, Boris Nemtsov, and other opposition politicians, civil activists, journalists, and lawyers.

- Involvement of political figures, businessmen, and parastatal entities close to the Putin regime in corruption that allowed them to enrich themselves at the expense of the Russian people. As Section 241 suggests, the Russian political elite has developed a sophisticated system of kleptocracy in which public assets are controlled (and regularly plundered) by a small circle of people close to Putin.

We, therefore, suggest that in compiling the report, the US administration apply the following three criteria:

1. The person named is close to the Russian regime, measured by his or her involvement in planning, ordering, preparing, financing, executing, or otherwise supporting the aggressive, corrupt, or criminal actions noted above; or
2. The person's fortune has been made through corrupt commercial operations with the Putin regime for the sake of personal gain; or
3. The person has held assets for Putin in what appears to be a corrupt fashion, even if he or she personally is not involved in the actions mentioned above, or his or her known personal fortune is not great enough to be considered of "oligarch" scale.

Earned wealth in itself should not be regarded as objectionable. Russians who have pursued the American (indeed, universal) dream of personal enrichment through outstanding entrepreneurship should be appreciated, not penalized. Further, formal rank is not dispositive. As the Panama Papers have revealed, often the big crooks are little known and have no official rank.

It is critical that persons are named in the Kremlin Report only on the basis of reliable information. Fortunately, the Kremlin political class, Putin, his friends, and their businesses have been extensively studied by credible researchers. The sources are many and the possibilities to cross check them for quality are ample. Plenty of disinformation exists, but with sufficient knowledge of how to assess sources, disinformation can be disregarded.

What Categories Should the Kremlin Report Include?

Applying the criteria discussed above, the senior political figures, oligarchs, and parastatal entities in the Russian Federation linked to the Kremlin—those people intended to be listed in the Kremlin Report—are best grouped into seven categories:

1. Senior political figures, parastatal entities, or business people responsible for aggressive, corrupt, or criminal operations within and outside the Russian Federation as noted above.

    a   We note a sub-category of oligarchs and others working with the Kremlin to advance aggressive foreign actions, such as organizing mercenary forces in Ukraine and Syria, or advancing cyber-warfare/disinformation, and recommend their inclusion;

2. Putin's close circle of contemporary friends from St. Petersburg, with whom he has done business since the early 1990s. They are commonly called his cronies and are well identified. The US government and European Union (EU) have already designated a number of them in the Ukraine-related sanctions;

3. Golden children. To a considerable extent, cronies have transferred their wealth to their children, who in some cases have become top executives. These people appear to have become full-fledged cronies in their own right;

4. Personal friends of Putin who hold considerable wealth for him. Some have been revealed by the Panama Papers and Russian Forbes;

5. The popularly acclaimed "oligarchs," who are big businessmen profiting greatly from direct business with the Kremlin. Some of these individuals are co-owners of companies with cronies. Others have operated as fronts for Kremlin leaders.

    a.   Note: Russia's wealthy businessmen should not be presumed to warrant listing simply by virtue of their wealth. Many made their fortunes before Putin and, to survive, are forced to pay large tributes to the Kremlin. Including such persons in the Kremlin Report would not appear consistent with the intent of Section 241;

6. Corrupt state enterprise managers who owe their positions to their close personal relations with Putin and utilize their positions for gross larceny; and

7. The relevant parastatal entities that are companies owned by the people noted in category six.

The preparation of the Kremlin Report will be a labor-intensive project. It is worth the effort because, among other things, it would demonstrate that whatever speculation exists to the contrary, the Trump administration, like previous US administrations, will respond with determination to counter Russian aggression against the United States, our European allies, and Russia's neighbors—Ukraine and Georgia. Thus far, the administration appears to be taking Russia sanctions seriously, judging by the guidance for CAATSA implementation, which it recently issued. It is our hope, and expectation, that the administration will show the requisite commitment to preparation of a strong, credible report as called for by CAATSA's Section 241.

Awaiting the Enemy's Corpse

First published on March 26th, 2021

The relationship between Russia and China represents a unique geopsychological case in the annals of world history. The Chinese have been masterful at playing on Russia's vain "elite" and the very real vulnerabilities that surfaced when the nation lost the Cold War, its empire, and its status as a global superpower. The suddenly popular—at least to those within and close to the power structures—"Eurasianism" took an ideological backseat and functioned as a way to take umbrage at the West. For the Russian "elite," it served as a kind of psychological buffer at certain critical times in its relations with the West. Aleksandr Blok's Scythians, with their slanted, hungry eyes, turned their formidable Asian physiognomy to the always alluring but always hated West and looked ready to pounce.

Little by little, this mask, which had no connection whatsoever with the Asia of today, began to attach itself permanently and the Russian "elite" had no other physiognomy left. The Chinese understood this all too well. They responded skeptically to the Russians and their attempts to ingratiate themselves. Although Chinese leaders kept everything on a professional level, one could not help but notice a certain amount of condescension and disdain.

"The Holy Asiope Alliance between Hu and Pu is an alliance between a rabbit and a boa constrictor"—a quote from about fifteen years ago from yours truly. "It will inevitably lead to our little Pu, and to all of us as well, being completely and totally Hu-ized. We simply have not been paying attention. We were so busy trying to recruit vassals in our 'near abroad' that we didn't realize that we were the ones becoming someone else's 'near abroad.'" "Pan Mongolism—the name is monstrous yet it caresses our ear."[3]

---

3   A quote from a Solovyov poem.

At the St. Petersburg Economic Forum in May of 2014, the Vice President of the People's Republic of China, Li Yuanchao, offered some direct, cogent advice to the leader of the Russian World: "Your lands are abundant and magnificent. But you do not run them with any discipline. The hard-working Chinese will take over and establish its Order Ordained by God."

As the number of threats the Kremlin has issued towards Ukraine has increased in recent years, a rather tempting opportunity has arisen for Beijing. The Chinese have been able to nudge along any of the more hesitant barbarians in Russia towards taking that last, fateful step, a move that would open up a whole range of brilliant prospects for China no matter how events unfold on the ground.

Scenario 1

With relative impunity Putin is able to occupy significant swaths of Ukrainian territory. The United States limits itself to an official condemnation (calling Putin a "killer," yet again) and another round of targeted sanctions that do not result in total economic war. Macron rushes to Moscow on a humanitarian peacekeeping mission meant to cement the Kremlin's military successes. If this comes to pass after the seven years of talk, negotiations, admonitions, forums, and formats we have seen, the result will be the complete collapse of the security system on the European continent. From that moment on, everyone in Europe will have to play by Russian rules and Russian rules only. For the US, this will signify more than a loss of status in Europe or the end of NATO as we know it. Two other entities will also cease to exist: the US as a global superpower and "the West" as a political concept.

The US would still remain a noticeable, albeit somewhat neutered economic giant on the world stage, but who then would believe any of their political, let alone military, assurances? I am referring to the Indo-Pacific region in particular. India? Japan? Australia? All of Washington's ambitious plans to counter China by forming the Quad Alliance would come to naught. The Chinese would quickly take advantage of the resulting geopolitical power vacuum and, with nothing to stop them, begin defiantly making their monumental visions a reality. The leadership had originally left these plans for the next generation (Taiwan, strategic restricted waters, disputed islands, etc.) China would also change its tone in trade negotiations with the US.

On August 23rd, 1939, the icebreaker "Adolf Hitler" was launched from Stalin's shipyards to carry out the historic global mission assigned to it—the destruction of the democratic West. By the summer of 1940 the vessel was very close to accomplishing this mission. These days Moscow and Beijing view the democratic West in almost the same way that Moscow and Berlin did 80 years ago, if not worse. The difference is that this time Moscow will not be the end beneficiary of the project; it will instead serve as the plan-ner—and the executor—in the form of the pirate schooner "Vladimir Putin," whose mission it is to break the West psychologically.

Scenario 2

Washington understands perfectly well everything I have outlined above. No matter how ferociously Kremlin agents/useful bourgeois idiots such as Kerry, Simes, Graham and Rodzhansky resist, the deep state will close ranks. The US will move to place horrendous sanctions on Russia (banning it from SWIFT, enacting an oil embargo, and arresting the so-called "Russian trillion"). The Americans will also provide a tremendous amount of sup-port (military, economic, political, etc.) to Ukraine as it battles the aggres-sor. Putin's military operation will sputter and fail. His closest advisors will remove him from office—those who despise him for getting them into this mess and those who despise him for not seeing it through to "a victory."

With the mafia boss now gone, it would remain nothing but a scorched patch of political earth and intensifying internal conflicts over property own-ership. It would be every man for himself. In this chaotic atmosphere of law-lessness, we would hear increasing talk from Beijing of the serious threats now posed to the safety and lives of millions of Chinese-speaking tractor operators, miners, and businessmen, not to mention the triad fighters resid-ing in the vast expanses of Siberia and the Far East.

The swift deployment of a limited number of polite little yellow men (to restore order) would be enthusiastically welcomed by the overwhelming majority of multi-national laborers.

A series of local referendums would follow organically. After the people exercise their right to vote, Siberia, the Far East, and the Holy Northern Sea (Baikal) would return to their native port—the Yuan Empire. It would be a wonderful gift to comrade Xi on the occasion of his anointing as leader for life and perhaps even founder of a new Chinese dynasty. As comrade Li once promised us, the industrious Chinese will restore the Mandate of Heaven in the Unified state of Great Eurasia.

***

The stakes are huge for the Chinese. They have already comfortably settled in to watch with curiosity from atop their famous fence—to see which enemy corpse will float past them first.

If the West Falters

First published on January 1st, 2022

On December 31, 2021, Ukraine's Foreign Minister Dmytro Kuleba nailed his historic tweet to the front door of the White House in Washington, DC.

> "Ukraine has been defending itself from ongoing Russian aggression for almost eight years now. All without being a NATO member. We are capable of defending ourselves. If the West falters and chooses appeasement, we will still defend ourselves, our right to exist and choose our own future."

> "Україна вже майже вісім років захищається від російської агресії, що триває. Попри те, що не є членом НАТО. Ми здатні захищатися. Якщо Захід похитнеться та обере умиротворення, майбутнє будемо захищати себе, своє право на існування і власне майбутнє."

The tweet was read in Washington just as Biden and his advisors were preparing for a call to Zelensky scheduled for January 2nd.

Once the tone and content of the December 30th discussion between the presidents of the United States and the Russian Federation were leaked to the press, we all knew what Biden was going to say to Zelensky in his scheduled call: "I have good news, Vladimir. It looks like I have been able to stop Putin from invading Ukraine. But now you have to do your part. Kiss the villain's hand and agree to his interpretation of the Minsk Agreements. Yes, yes. Oh, and agree to this special status he wants for the Donetsk and Luhansk regions, to the Steinmeier Formula, and to elections run by the occupiers. At the end of the day, as far as I am aware, we are talking only about a little bit of autonomy for one of Ukraine's provinces. You and I cannot risk subjecting mankind to a global war over such an insignificant matter. Not least because the American voter will not understand it."

No, this is not a deliberate betrayal or an attempt at appeasement. What we are seeing, first and foremost, is clear proof that not a single American politician or specialist in the field understands Putin's maniacal obsession with his interpretation of the Minsk Agreements. He even railroaded Biden into muttering something positive about the agreements to the press in Geneva. From that time on, every American visiting Moscow has been forced to pledge his allegiance to these Minsk Agreements.

And after the lobotomy session that took place via video conference on December 7th, Biden has made sure to memorize terms such as "special status" and "Steinmeier." For Putin, the most efficient and reliable way to undermine Ukrainian statehood is to gain legitimacy for the terrorist staging grounds of Donetsk and Luhansk within the Ukrainian legal and political realms, without making any changes whatsoever to the regions. He doesn't need Donetsk and Luhansk; they are mere crumbs. What he needs is the whole of Ukraine. Many in Washington would breathe a sigh of relief if Zelensky took Biden's warnings to heart. He would then bear full responsibility for everything that occurred thereafter. The Americans, after all, cannot be more pro-Ukraine than the Ukrainians themselves. But now that will never happen.

The Kremlin propagandists went into their standard mode of hysterics—"We are on the edge, it will take only five minutes for a missile to reach Moscow, we will never make concessions, we will tear you all apart, we have hypersonic missiles, give us a Zone up to the Adriatic Littoral." The point? For the most part it's to force Biden to join them in pressuring Ukraine to finally accept Putin's Invitation to a Beheading (*Nabokov*).

But then Kuleba stymied the Kremlin's plans and those of its agents in Washington with a single threatening tweet. On Monday, Congress will return to Washington after its Christmas recess and it won't interpret Kuleba's response from December 31st and Zelensky's from January 2nd as cries for help from weak men. It will see them as evidence that Ukraine is sure of itself and its cause. Ukraine is reminding the West as it heads into retirement just who and for whom (not just for itself!) the country is fighting. We know what is now on History's scales, What is, in the world, going now (*Akhmatova*).

The US Must Arm Ukraine Now, Before It's Too Late

First published on August 18th, 2022

The manifesto published in "The Hill" on August 17th, signed by more than 20 retired ambassadors and generals, is a remarkable political document. The language is simply brilliant, reminding one of some of the best of Churchill's wartime speeches. It has the potential to exert considerable influence on the course of this 4th World War that has been unleashed by the Kremlin's paranoiac against Western civilization. One of the Free World's fundamental weaknesses is that it has not had an agreed-upon leader in decades. This role has traditionally been filled by the person occupying the Oval Office in the White House. But the leaders who met with Putin in Helsinki and Geneva fell far short of impressing the dictator. He looked them both up and down and found them wanting. The same was true for their predecessor who famously said, "Tell Vladimir I will have more flexibility in a second term." Vladimir made good use of that message by annexing Crimea during the second term of the 44th occupant of the White House.

That is why sixteen angry American men and four angry American women assumed the mantle of collective leader of the Free World. A little over a year ago, this same group of influential government and military officials offered a blunt assessment of the US's disastrous showing at the summit in Geneva: "Putin got exactly what he wanted from Biden in Geneva."

Drawing on support from the public at large, Congress, and prominent Cabinet members such as Lloyd Austin and Antony Blinken, the group was able to overcome the administration's tendency to appease the aggressor. The decadent, pampered West should consider itself lucky that a great nation such as Ukraine is willing to protect it at such a perilous moment from the Rashist scourge.

"Ukraine was able to win the battle for Kyiv with unsophisticated weaponry. If we were to send aircraft, missile defense systems, state-of-the-art artillery, and MLRS, we wouldn't have to defend every inch of territory covered by Article 5. Ukraine will do it all for us, and that includes delivering the bloody dictator to the Hague. There he will utter his last words," argued Daniel Fried, John Herbst, and others, addressing the Biden administration.

It seems that their message was finally heeded. The Biden administration approved a major military aid package that truly changed the rules of the game on the battlefield. Secretary of Defense Lloyd Austin delivered a speech on April 25th in which he characterized the US's goals in the war as three-fold: "First, victory for Ukraine. Second, its territorial integrity must be fully restored. And finally, weakening Russia to such a point that it is never able to commit such acts of aggression again." Austin has repeated these three goals several times since then, but every time, the next morning another high-ranking Biden official, National Security Advisor Jake Sullivan, has done his best to undermine the general's words: "Our goal is to keep Ukraine from losing while preventing an escalation of the conflict or a direct confrontation with a nuclear power." On a practical level, every time the Biden administration made a decision about a new military aid package, Sullivan was able to limit the scale and types of weapons to be delivered to levels insufficient for Ukraine to achieve victory. The (new) collective leader of the Free World assesses the situation as it stands today in the same manifesto:

"Although the Biden administration has successfully rallied US allies and provided substantial military assistance to Ukraine's valiant armed forces, it has failed to produce a satisfactory strategic narrative which enables governments to maintain public support for the NATO engagement over the long term. By providing aid sufficient to produce a stalemate, but not enough to roll back Russian territorial gains, the Biden administration may be unintentionally seizing defeat from the jaws of victory. Out of an over-abundance of caution about provoking Russian escalation (conventional as well as nuclear), we are in effect ceding the initiative to the Russian President and reducing the pressure on Moscow to halt its aggression."

It's debatable whether it was intentional or not that the Biden administration (via Sullivan's efforts) is dooming Ukraine to defeat after it had already won a strategic victory. Nonetheless, the authors are addressing not only the administration. We see that they are also appealing to the American public, pointing out that the security and fate of the United States hang in the balance as well. They reject Sullivan's hypocritical "warnings" and the dozens of Putin agents and useful bourgeois idiots in the American media parroting his rhetoric. On the contrary, they say, the US supplying Ukraine with the weaponry needed to win the war eliminates (not exacerbates!) the threat of a military confrontation in Central Europe with a nuclear power. It also saves the lives of thousands of American troops who would have had to fight on NATO member state territory. Putin has never hidden his seething hatred of the West or his desire to avenge the Soviet Union's defeat in the Third (Cold) World War. And now we see the incredibly motivated Ukrainian military defending not only its own country but every inch of Article 5 NATO territory as well. The only military in the world capable of carrying out this historic mission. If the US were to snatch a well-deserved and hard-won Victory from Ukraine, it would not only qualify as the vilest of betrayals of a heroic ally but a catastrophic blow to its own national security as well. It would also mark the end of the US as a major player on the world stage, much to the delight of every dictator and enemy of freedom across the globe. I am sure that the American people, Congress, and the Biden administration will heed the words of its best citizens. Ukraine will receive the weaponry it needs to achieve a decisive victory over the Empire of Egregious Evil.

A New Steinmeier Formula

First published on October 28th, 2022

Ribbentrop (Lavrov) will be reminded of a lot when he faces an international tribunal in Mariupol for the most egregious Russian war criminals, including his jubilant and cynical assessment of the Minsk Accords: "Zelensky will never be able to rid himself of the noose of the Minsk Accords and the Steinmeier Formula!"

The surname of this Foreign Minister (and subsequent President of Germany) has long served as a meme for many Ukrainians, a symbol of the West's weakness and its shameful capitulation to Rashist aggression. But Steinmeier's recent arrival in Kyiv was perceived as the courageous act of an honorable man. I am referring above all to his intellectual courage, a quality no less important than physical courage. Steinmeier's moment of clarity, leading him to condemn both his own illusions and misperceptions and those of his party vis-a-vis the Putin regime, has spread far and wide across German society.

Evidence of Putin's monstrous crimes is causing a great deal of shame in Germany over its enduring attempts to "empathize with Putin." It seems that decades of denazification and atonement for Hitler's misdeeds have made their mark on the collective German consciousness; we are witnessing before our very eyes a tectonic shift in German foreign policy.

For too long Putin and, alas, the people subservient to him, have violated all the laws of God and man and crossed every imaginable boundary. The G7 summit on October 11th was called as a direct response to the heinous attacks on Ukraine's civilian infrastructure launched two days before. This response on the part of the civilized world was first and foremost a moral one, but its political ramifications were considerable.

During the Group of Seven meetings the group expanded to the Group of Eight. President Zelensky of Ukraine essentially took part in a conference call with major world leaders of the Free World.

The historic statement issued at the summit on Ukraine begins with these memorable lines:

We, the leaders of the Group of Seven (G7), convened today with Ukraine's President Volodymyr Zelenskyy. Our meeting took place against the backdrop of the most recent missile attacks against civilian infrastructure and cities across Ukraine, leading to the death of innocent civilians. We condemn these attacks in the strongest possible terms and recall that indiscriminate attacks on innocent civilian populations constitute a war crime. We will hold President Putin and those responsible to account.

The G7 member states also offered their support for Zelensky's Plan for a Just Peace, which contains the following four demands:

1. The territorial integrity of Ukraine must be completely restored;
2. Legal and military guarantees for Ukraine's security must be provided moving forward;
3. Ukraine's economy must be restored using reparations imposed on the Russian Federation;
4. Russian war criminals must be brought to justice

These demands are now no longer merely a part of Vladimir Zelensky's plan. They represent an ultimatum given to the Russian Federation by the Group of Eight.

After every world war (and we are now bearing witness to and participating in a fourth one), a new framework for European and global security is built. And it is the victorious powers who do the building. As for what is transpiring right now, the victorious powers will be Ukraine, the UK, and the US.

Ukraine's heroic efforts in countering Rashist aggression have motivated and rallied the West at a time when it seemed weak, hedonistic, and lacking all political will. It looked as if the West no longer cared if it played a role in global politics. And so we saw Ukraine assume the mantle of Leader of the Free World that the West had let fall to the ground. The country's leadership has not only completely altered the course of the war in Ukraine but the geopolitical landscape in Central Europe, the entire post-Soviet space, and the Far East (!) as well. US General Ben Hodges had it right when he said in one of his interviews, "China will never forgive Putin for shaking the West from its slumber."

The price the allies will pay for this collective victory is incomparable to the one Ukraine faces—thousands and thousands of human lives. The only way to limit the losses the Ukrainians will endure as it defends not only the security and freedoms of its homeland but those of the entire Free World as well is to guarantee the nation receives immediate and maximized shipments of the offensive weapons it needs to destroy the Russian alignment of forces.

The President of Germany was shaken by what he saw in Ukraine. Upon his return to Berlin, he articulated a new Steinmeier Formula: "Russia's war in Ukraine has reduced European security to ashes. It is an attack on everything that we Germans stand for. Germany and Russia are now in direct confrontation."

Future historians will refer to this speech from October 28th as a turning point in German foreign policy and rank it up there with the best of Churchill's wartime rhetoric.

That is, of course, if the necessary number of "Leopard 2" tanks are delivered to our heroic Ukrainian soldiers as soon as humanly possible.

On the Death of the Patriarch

First published on January 12th, 2023

Henry Kissinger's finest hour was his clandestine trip to Peking in July 1971 to meet with China's Premier Zhou Enlai. During the meeting the two coordinated President Nixon's visit to China the following February. It is not hyperbole to state that the Nixon-Mao summit determined the outcome of the Third (Cold) World War. The US and China used the occasion to establish their de-facto military and political alliance, after which the USSR was doomed. It simply floundered about for another two decades in a mindless state of stagnation.

But today, as the world bids farewell to a towering statesman whom I had the honor of knowing personally, another of his intellectual feats comes to mind, one which he accomplished on the eve of his 100th (!) birthday. Kissinger spent the last thirty-odd years of his life engaged in a tireless struggle against NATO's expansion. As for Ukraine, he recommended again and again that the country undergo "Finlandization." This position was completely organic for him. Whether he was motivated by pragmatic or cynical reasons depends on one's point of view.

The old man was looking to repeat his brilliant maneuver from the 1970s, only this time he wanted to get the Russians on his side in the imminent conflict between the US and China. For that to work, he of course had to take into consideration certain "concerns" of Kremlin leaders.

But then, in 2022, Kissinger had a significant change of heart.

"Ukraine has become a major state in Central Europe for the first time in modern history. Aided by its allies and inspired by its President, Volodymyr Zelensky, Ukraine has stymied the Russian conventional forces which have been overhanging Europe since the second world war. This process has mooted the original issues regarding Ukraine's membership in NATO. Ukraine has acquired one of the largest and most effective land armies in

Europe, equipped by America and its allies. The alternative of neutrality is no longer meaningful, especially after Sweden joined NATO."

I consider Kissinger's words here the last bequest of an extraordinary thinker to the politicians of the West. The author's sense of responsibility and regret for many years of "considering concerns" is truly palpable. The 75th anniversary NATO summit in Washington is the perfect opportunity to make good on Kissinger's bequest. Future historians will then justifiably regard this unique individual as the architect behind the West's victory over the forces of Darkness in both the Third and Fourth World Wars.

Without Making the West Bleed

First published on March 12th, 2023

The political solidarity of Ukraine's allies was on prominent display recently at several high-level meetings (the Munich Security Conference, the EU summit, and Biden's visits to Kyiv and Warsaw). The Ramstein format allowed for significant progress on weapon shipments, including armored vehicles, and the doubling of the radius of HIMARS firepower.

And yet there's still a sense of ambiguity and of things left unsaid, if you will, when it comes to the allies' relationship. It would not be wise to march into a decisive battle with that kind of cloud hanging over the participants, especially when that battle will determine, and here I am not exaggerating in the slightest, the fate of 21st century mankind. The allies need to be completely open with one another even if that means saying certain unpleasant things to friends.

Let's start with an old standard that grates on the nerves. Even the most robust statements of support for Ukraine issued by Western politicians are inevitably accompanied by the following proviso: "And yet we cannot allow the conflict to escalate. Therefore a direct confrontation between NATO and the Russian Federation is simply out of the question."

Who is the intended audience for the West's incessant appeals to "refrain from escalating the conflict?" Putin has already escalated the conflict as far as he could with his concentrated missile attacks on Ukrainian cities resulting in the genocide of the Ukrainian people. In response, the West has justifiably established a special tribunal to investigate the ongoing crimes against humanity being committed by Putin and his accomplices. At the same time, this call for restraint essentially renders the victim of these crimes helpless. It prevents Ukraine from effectively defending its citizenry from lethal missile strikes. Ukraine either does not receive long-range missiles and aircraft or it receives them with the condition that no weapon manufactured in the West be used to strike within Russian territory.

How could they *not* be used to strike airfields from which Russian aircraft take off with missiles intended to destroy Ukrainian cities?

What is the West afraid of? Putin escalating things to nuclear war? To be sure, nuclear blackmail has served Putin well for over fifteen years as an instrument of foreign policy. But at some point during the war the US finally realized it could not keep backing down at every empty bluster issued by an opportunist from a country inferior in every way. The Americans made it abundantly clear just what would happen to Putin personally if he were to attempt to employ tactical nuclear weapons.

We soon saw that Putin was no suicide bomber dreaming of an afterlife in heaven with seventy-two virgins to greet him. He feels perfectly comfortable with just Kabayeva, lounging on a golden toilet in their luxurious, gaudy palace; he seems to greatly appreciate this more earthy way of life. So just why is the West so frightened by the prospect of a NATO-Russia military engagement? Let's say Ukraine begins receiving those shipments of F-16 fighter jets, causing Putin some anxiety. In a desperate move, he decides to launch a (conventional) air strike on an airfield in Romania or Poland. Great news! NATO would finally have a reason to act on the warning it has issued at least a thousand times: we will be steadfast and ferocious in our defense of every inch of sacrosanct territory covered by Article V of our charter. A war against the "second best in the world" Russian army would be over in a few days at most. Tens of thousands of Ukrainian lives would be saved, lives that were surely doomed were these soldiers to fight the Putin horde alone.

But over the course of those few days of war, hundreds of NATO soldiers would also die, possibly along with a number of European civilians. This is an unacceptable outcome for the West, which knows exactly what Ukraine is doing and has already done for the Free World, at the cost of innumerable lives. Stoltenberg said it best: "Yes, we are paying money for the cause but the Ukrainians are paying in blood. If they falter and Putin succeeds, we will also pay in blood."

The West has made up its mind. Sure, in principle it would like to see Ukraine win the war and have its territorial integrity restored. But it wants it to happen without any NATO bloodshed. Ukraine has no choice but to accept this position. The Ukrainian counteroffensive will take place as planned. But first the country needs to receive the ATACMS shipments that are absolutely crucial for its success. These missiles can reach the entirety of the Crimean peninsula. Ukraine also needs state-of-the-art military aircraft in sufficient numbers. There must be absolute clarity on these issues among the allies.

A White House Divided on Russia and Ukraine?

First published on September 8th, 2023 with Fred Starr

A prime task of Russia's State Security Service (FSB), successor to the KGB, is to devise and execute active measures in the sphere of foreign relations. During Russian President Vladimir Putin's era, one of the most successful initiatives to arise from its headquarters in the infamous Lubianka in Moscow, has been the proposal to relaunch Track II (unofficial and backchannel) negotiations between Moscow and Washington.

When Putin concluded that official diplomatic contacts were failing to produce the results he wanted, he embraced the FSB's proposals to establish an informal working group of retired US and Russian officials and experts who are "close to decision-making centers." Meeting in picturesque locales and in a relaxed atmosphere that excluded neckties but could include swimming trunks, the respected participants, so it was thought, would be able to reach unexpected but useful conclusions that could then be couched in diplomatic language and transmitted privately to key policy makers.

Had this not worked successfully two generations ago when the Dartmouth Conferences opened new avenues in arms control? Back then, however, such talks had been initiated by distinguished citizens on both sides. Could Putin now use the same formula to advance his own programs? Everyone in official Moscow was extremely pleased with the concept, and its implementation came quickly.

To head the US delegation, the Kremlin would draw from the narrow circle of Americans whom it had judged to be agents of influence at the top of the US political beau monde and, at the same time, sympathetic to Moscow's concerns. It would be led by an individual with long and positive links with the Kremlin. This person would be surrounded with an entourage of other Americans known to be sympathetic to Moscow—the kind of folks Vladimir Lenin once described as "useful bourgeois idiots."

Guided by these considerations, the organizers at the FSB's head-quarters in Lubianka named Army General Viacheslav Trubnikov, director of the foreign intelligence service, to head the Russian team; and Thomas Graham, former senior director for Russia on the National Security Council staff, to head the US "experts." One of their early meetings took place on the Finnish island of Boisto, halfway between Helsinki and the Russian border, in June, 2014.

This session gave rise to the conceptual contours of the Minsk Accords, which Washington and Moscow jointly imposed on Ukraine. This agreement was nothing less than a modern version of the infamous Molotov-Ribbentrop pact of 1939, which specified Adolf Hitler and Joseph Stalin's future spheres of control. Falling into line, Putin's Minister of Foreign Affairs, Sergei Lavrov, would assert eight times that "we shall never allow Ukraine to get off the hook of the Minsk Accords."

Nine years later, Putin's trumpet again summoned the US pundits to battle. Along with Graham, these included Richard Haas, then in his last years as president of the Council of Foreign Relations, and Charles Kupchan, professor of international affairs at Georgetown University. On April 24, 2023, Graham and his colleagues met in New York with Lavrov, who had come to town to chair (however ironically) the UN's Security Council. As NBC reported, this meeting took place with the knowledge of the White House.

Graham and his group then briefed Jake Sullivan, US President Joe Biden's director of the National Security Council, on the results of the meeting and on the working group's further plans. We note that, for three months, the NSC maintained a stoic silence on the meeting's existence and the group's activities.

A denial finally came on July 27th. On that day, the Moscow Times published an extensive interview with an "anonymous" head of the US negotiating group, who was visiting Moscow. The lengthy article was entitled "Former US Official Shares Details of Secret 'Track 1.5' Diplomacy with Moscow." It featured an extended interview with the leader of America's unorthodox team of self-styled diplomats. Though not identified by name, Thomas Graham waxed eloquent:

> Sitting across from senior Kremlin officials and advisers, it was apparent that the greatest issue was that the Russians were unable to articulate what exactly they wanted and needed. They don't know how to define victory or defeat. In

fact, some of the elites to whom we spoke had never wanted the war in the first place, even saying it had been a complete mistake. But now they're at war—suffering a humiliating defeat is not an option for these guys.

Graham added: "It was here that we made clear that the US was prepared to work constructively with Russian national security concerns." In doing so, he broke from the official US line of squeezing Russia financially and isolating it internationally so as to prevent it from continuing its war against Ukraine.

An attempt to isolate and cripple Russia to the point of humiliation or collapse would make negotiating almost impossible—we are already seeing this in the reticence from Moscow officials," Graham said. "In fact, we emphasized that the US needs, and will continue to need, a strong enough Russia to create stability along its periphery. The US wants a Russia with strategic autonomy in order for the US to advance diplomatic opportunities in Central Asia. We in the US have to recognize that total victory in Europe could harm our interests in other areas of the world. Russian power is not necessarily a bad thing.

During our discussions, it became evident that Ukraine's chances of regaining its occupied territories were extremely slim. Crimea remains a particularly contentious issue, as Ukraine asserts its intent to reclaim the region which Russia annexed in 2014. If Russia thought it might lose Crimea, it would almost certainly resort to [using] tactical nuclear weapons.

Graham's readiness to succumb to Putin's nuclear blackmail is astonishing, but yet more so is his readiness then to propose US policies based on it. Never mind that he was then, and still is, employed by Henry Kissinger, and has no formal relationship with the US government.

Yet he confidently reported to the Russians that Washington would offer to help conduct fair referendums in the Russian-occupied territories of Donetsk, Luhansk, Kherson and Zaporizhzhia, in which residents would vote on whether they wished to be part of Ukraine or Russia. That tens of thousands of those residents had already fled or been killed by the Russian army attests either to his ignorance or cynicism, or both.

"The United States has not requested any official or former officials to open a back channel and is not seeking such a channel. Nor are we passing any messages through others. When we say nothing about Ukraine without Ukraine, we mean it."

Sullivan's claim that he did not even know about the Track II negotiations with the Kremlin might have been reassuring, except for one problem: he lied. We now know that he had been thoroughly briefed about all the details of the meeting that Graham and his two "useful idiots" held with Lavrov on April 24th in New York.

Finally, the most important thing: The above-mentioned published statements by Graham correspond closely with the concept of the war in Ukraine that both Sullivan and CIA director William Burns had been championing within the US administration for a year and a half. Not once have either of these two officials called for the return of all occupied territories to Ukraine, let alone uttered the words "Victory for Ukraine."

For them, America's objective in this major European war is not for Ukraine to win but to assure that Russia is not defeated. Devoted to this goal, they have delayed the delivery to Ukraine of weapons that are essential if it is to achieve a decisive victory, and even for its survival as a state.

Ukrainians are dying today because the Biden administration, paralyzed by the Burns-Sullivan philosophy of appeasement, refuses to act. Is it not high time for Speaker of the House Kevin McCarthy to do his job and bring Burns and Sullivan under oath to account for their private and secretive talks with Putin?

Is CIA Director Bill Burns Helping Ukraine to Win or Blocking It?

September 23rd, 2023 with Fred Starr

Almost 600 days of Russia's war in Ukraine have given rise to almost 600 days of confrontation between pro-Ukrainian and Kremlin-appeasing groups within the US administration.

The good news is that friends of Ukraine have largely succeeded in overcoming the artificial and self-destructive taboo against supporting Ukraine that the US has imposed on itself. The bad news is that—each time—Kyiv's American skeptics seem to succeed in significantly slowing down US support.

Unacknowledged in large parts of official Washington is the reality that thousands of Ukrainian soldiers and civilians have had to pay for this procrastination with their lives. Had there been a hundred or more F-16 fighter jets in the Ukrainian skies a year ago, this cursed war would now be history.

Meanwhile, the US's puzzling taboo has deliberately tied the hands of the victims of criminal aggression. The US press has reported in detail on how Russia invaded Ukraine, is destroying its cities and villages, and is daily murdering civilians with rockets launched from Russian territory. Yet Washington has effectively prohibited Ukraine from delivering answering strikes on the sources of Russia's bombings.

Not one US official has publicly admitted that this line has been adopted. Worse, some act as if it doesn't exist. While his colleagues in the White House have dragged their feet on providing Ukraine with military aircraft, Secretary of State Antony Blinken has unambiguously asserted Ukraine's right to utilize any weapon at its disposal to expel the occupiers, including strikes on the territory of the aggressor.

An illuminating article published earlier this summer in Newsweek—"Exclusive: The CIA's Blind Spot about Ukraine War" by William Arkin, revealed the origins and inner workings of the confused US approach.

At Biden's behest, CIA Director William Joseph Burns established direct communication with Russian President Vladimir Putin in Moscow as early as in November 2021, that is three months before Russia launched its full-scale attack on Ukraine.

"In some ironic ways . . . the meeting was highly successful," a senior US intelligence official told Newsweek. "The United States would not fight directly nor seek regime change, the Biden administration pledged. Russia would limit its assault to Ukraine and act in accordance with unstated but well-understood guidelines for secret operations."

But, according to Newsweek, "Once Russian forces poured into Ukraine, the United States had to quickly shift gears. The CIA, like the rest of the US intelligence community, had misread Russia's military capacity and Ukraine's resilience as Russia failed to take Kyiv and withdrew from the north."

Nevertheless, certain clandestine rules of the road apparently agreed to by Burns and Putin were adhered to by the US side. Washington would prohibit Ukraine from carrying out strikes on Russian territory. And, in return, speaking as if for all NATO, Burns sought and gained a promise from the dictator not to attack NATO member countries.

Burns met with Russian foreign intelligence chief Sergei Naryshkin in Ankara in November 2022 and then is believed to have briefed Ukraine's President Volodymyr Zelensky about his "non-agreement" with the Russians.

Far from criticizing Burns, Arkin emoted on the CIA's difficulties in keeping an eye on the increasingly unruly Ukrainians, who repeatedly attempted to deliver strikes on targets both in Russian occupied Crimea and Russia itself.

Naryshkin revealed that he and Burns "thought about and deliberated on what should be done about Ukraine" in a lengthy phone call on June 30, initiated by the US side.

Over the 560+ days of Russia's so-called "special military operation," and tens of thousands of documented war crimes, instances of torture, shootings and rape, Burns and the CIA have remained silent on Russia, while apparently issuing threats to Ukraine. On July 5th, a CIA spokesperson warned that if Kyiv continued acts of sabotage within Russia it could have "disastrous consequences."

What other catastrophic consequences are the people in Burn's office expecting will occur through the fault of the Ukrainians?

All thinkable and unthinkable catastrophes have already happened as a result of the covert Burns-Putin deal. Yet Newsweek was beside itself with pride at Burns' diplomatic success and expressed anger at the Ukrainians for trying to defend their country by violating the "ground rules" that Burns was seeking to impose on them without their consent.

With Russia's war against Ukraine dragging on and on, and the Ukrainians eager to break through with the proper support of their supporters, should this cruel state of affairs be allowed to continue?

The bipartisan pro-Ukrainian majority in the post-vacation Congress would do well to organize hearings to which they should invite Blinken, Burns, Arkin and those sources in the CIA whom he cites in his article. They should also invite National Security Advisor Jake Sullivan, who has been singing in the same key as Burns.

The hearings should seek answers to the following questions:

1. Does there exist an agreement between the governments of the US and the Russian Federation about "rules of the road" for the Russo-Ukrainian war?
2. If so, why were Congress and the American people unaware of them until now?
3. If not, then on what basis is Burns imposing these "road rules" on Ukraine?
4. Should Congress regard Burns' actions as treasonous?

Burns and Sullivan live in a world where the great powers set the rules and small countries must humbly obey. So does Putin.

We do not have to live in such a world and accept the rules they seek to impose on us.

How the West Can and Must Triumph in World War IV

First published on October 15th, 2023

After those so-called "exercises" took place in Ryazan in September 1999, anyone with half a brain realized that the series of apartment block explosions on Russian soil had been organized by the Chekists who were de-facto running the country. To what end? To blame it all on the Chechens, start a war, and wipe out both Chechnya and Russia once and for all in their patriotic outhouses.

Twenty or so years later, a more mature Putin and Patrushev set their sights on a much grander piece of performance art—a monumental Victory over the West in a World War IV unleashed to avenge the USSR's defeat in World War III (the Cold War). Putin and Patrushev were absolutely convinced (and thus able to sway the whole upper leadership as well) that a unique opportunity had arisen to make their mark on world history and avenge the USSR's defeat all with one simple roll of the dice.

"Those dumb Yanks will back down if we threaten them with nuclear strikes and then give up the Baltic states," thought the wise men of the Kremlin. "Just like Chamberlain gave up Czechoslovakia and Obama gave up Syria after retreating from his own "red lines" without a single threat being issued."

"Gather your stuff and get the hell out of here," demanded Ryabkov, the fat-faced deputy minister, of twenty-eight NATO nations. "If you don't, you will face a cataclysm the likes of which your countries have never seen," the future Master of the Universe threatened.

Despite the West's massive economic and military superiority, the chance to humiliate it by sheer force of will and show the world how indecisive and feeble it was, was so beguiling and offered such astounding geopolitical dividends, that this sorry excuse for a fuhrer at the helm of this sorry excuse for an empire could not resist the temptation. The fate of the world was decided in February 2022 at the Battle of Hostomel. If Kyiv had fallen then, Putin might have appeared on the border with the Baltics and Poland, drunk on the afterglow of victory and waving his nuclear schlong to and fro. The West of spring 2022 might have flinched and the insane plan from P and P just might have prevailed.

Much has changed in the last year and a half. Ukraine performed a heroic feat, akin to the 300 Spartans of the Free World, by literally grabbing the hedonistic West by the scruff of its neck and dragging it back to the world stage. The US finally provided an appropriate response to Russia's nuclear blackmail by making it clear to Putin just what would happen to him personally if he so much as reached for a nuclear weapon. Putin has never doubted the West's superiority when it comes to conventional weapons. Now he dreams of a cease-fire in Ukraine which he will try to sell to his deep people as a fake "honorable draw."

But World War IV itself, unleashed on the West, has not come to an end. Standing in the shadows behind our hapless Petersburg thug is another ambitious nutjob. The Iranian Islamofascist regime came to the same strategic conclusion as their like-minded brethren in the Kremlin. If the task is to cripple a faltering United States from a spiritual standpoint and then toss it in the dustbin of world history, one must make a show of crushing one of its allies with utter impunity.

The Kremlin has called for about a dozen Eastern European NATO countries to return to the fold. The Ayatollahs have long wished for the destruction of Israel, a major non-NATO ally of the US.

The incredibly heinous terrorist attack which took place on October 7th was merely the first move in Tehran's intricate game of chess designed to exterminate the Jews in the Middle East once and for all. The unthinkable atrocities live-streamed to the whole world were committed in pursuit of a single goal—to force Israel to launch a ground operation to eradicate Hamas infrastructure and military personnel. When Israeli efforts to clear out the rubble and purge the underground tunnels of Gaza eventually get bogged down and the military begins to suffer significant losses, the handlers in Iran will dispatch a 50,000-strong Hezbollah horde of thugs to the north of the country. The premise was so simple and the intentions so obvious that this plan was thwarted the very next day—October 8—when the Leader of the Free World, the United States, finally awakened from its politically correct period of hibernation. Two carrier forces and some rather pointed words from Biden, Blinken, and Austin served as a persuasive argument for Hezbollah and its sponsors. They now limit themselves to frequent shelling and border raids, not daring to launch a full-scale invasion. Thanks to its powerful ally, Israel is free to concentrate on fully rooting out Hamas in Gaza without the distractions posed by other, rather serious threats.

It would seem, then, that conditions are extremely favorable for Israel at the moment. But let us consider what would happen the day after such a notional "victory." The Israeli military would suffer major losses and most hostages would likely be dead. A hue and cry would then be raised from both Islamic fascists and Western liberals concerning the "peaceful inhabitants" of Gaza and their suffering. Amidst all this, an unsolvable problem would arise—just what to do with these two million or so "peaceful inhabitants" the day after. Especially while the breeding ground of Islamist terror within Iran remains untouched and unpunished, free to continue training, funding, and arming Hamas-like groups throughout the Middle East.

It is the author's opinion that the allies (Israel and the US) must understand that there are more urgent matters to attend to in this full-scale war designed to destroy Israel than enacting revenge on Hamas. They could do with a slight adjustment to the sequence of their tactics. First, however, I would like to remind my readers of Secretary of State Tony Blinken's heartfelt words from October 12th concerning the nature of US-Israeli relations: "The message that I bring Israel is this: You may be strong enough on your own to defend yourself—but as long as America exists, you will never, ever have to. We will always be there, by your side." With those words, delivered in Jerusalem, in mind, I would like to propose an alternative scenario to the allies that would result in a decisive Victory for the West over its mortal enemies.

The US's two carrier forces together with the Israeli air force must conduct a devastating strike on Hezbollah before it is able to make good on its plans for a full-scale invasion of Israel. The strike must wipe out all Hezbollah military facilities as well as its leaders' upscale mansions in Beirut.

This would constitute a just response to the crimes Hezbollah has committed in the past and the ones it is on the verge of committing. Perhaps most of all, the strike represents an absolutely essential prerequisite for the allies to pursue its main objective—an airstrike on Iran. Iran makes no secret of the fact that the massive aerial assault capabilities it has supplied to Hezbollah, currently aimed directly at Israel, also act as a deterrent to keep the Jewish state from striking Iranian nuclear facilities. Israel has issued warning after warning that it intends to strike Iran the moment it looks close to obtaining a nuclear weapon. The US has also not ruled out using its military to solve the Iranian nuclear issue.

Not all that long ago, the Pentagon announced that, according to US intelligence, the ayatollahs are a mere two weeks away from commissioning their first nuclear warhead. There is no time to delay. Israel has long maintained that it is fully capable of carrying out a "nuclear castration" of Iran all on its own. But the world at large has heard loud and clear that Israel will "never, ever, have to act alone. America will always be there." This is especially relevant in our current environment when Israel can no longer go it alone.

The political and military leadership of Iran is conducting a war whose goal is the physical annihilation of the state of Israel and the complete moral destruction of the United States. It is more dangerous than ISIS and must be mercilessly exterminated. For that reason, targets for potential airstrikes within Iran, apart from all nuclear and missile production facilities, must also include key decision-making centers in the country (the ayatollahs all the way down the list, starting with the Supreme Leader, the leaders of the IRGC and the military, etc.)

The state of Israel simply does not possess any strategic territorial depth. And so every major war it is forced to fight ends up being a war for survival. In 1968, Israel conducted a preventive strike which led to a magnificent victory. In 1973, it refrained from such actions and found itself on the verge of disaster. This time around Israel has a powerful ally by its side. Israel, along with Ukraine, finds itself on the frontlines of a global war declared by the axis of absolute evil primarily on the United States of America. After the allies deliver two crushing, if you will, preventive strikes on Hezbollah and Iran, Hamas's main sponsors will disappear in an instant. Consequently, the delayed ground operation to root out its members will be conducted in a totally different political and psychological environment. What's more, with the Iranian Islamofascists gone, the question of what to do with Gaza in the future might elicit some real, constructive responses. Not only Gaza, but the Middle East as a whole will be able to continue enacting the positive changes stipulated by the Abraham Accords. The allies will have to strike Hezbollah and Iran eventually anyway. But conducting two successive strikes now would be much more effective from both a political and military standpoint than doing it after the IDF exhausts itself deep in the tunnels of Gaza.

Anything but War?

First published on January 12th, 2024

There was a period of time after the events of October 7th when I had memorized the messaging the White House was putting out concerning the status of our global war and could produce it word for word during my online media appearances. I could barely keep myself from shouting, "Damn, you're good, Piontkovsky, you're one good son of a bitch! You've finally become a speechwriter for the American political and military leadership."

Here is a favorite sentiment that General Lloyd Austin and I share:

"In both Israel and Ukraine, democracies are fighting ruthless foes who are out to annihilate them. Only firm American leadership can ensure that tyrants, thugs, and terrorists are not emboldened to commit more aggression and more atrocities."

These kind words from our 4-star general gained a foothold in the consciousness of their target audience when two carrier strike groups and an Ohio-class nuclear submarine were dispatched to the Middle East.

While this was happening, Tony Blinken was in Jerusalem, speaking with no less determination and perhaps even more passion. Here was his solemn promise to the Israelis: "As long as America exists, you will never ever have to fight your enemies alone. America will always be by your side."

So it would seem nothing is hindering the United States from providing Ukraine and Israel with the necessary aid so that together they can crush these genocidal tyrants, thugs, and terrorists.

But three months have now passed. Tony Blinken returned the other day from his most recent tour of the Middle East where he tried to persuade Israel to . . . apply the brakes, or, even better, finish up its operation in Gaza. Under no circumstances, he said, can things escalate in the north of Israel, resulting in a regional war.

What happened during these three months, then? The radical left wing of the US Democratic party happened. The so-called "progressives" and their brainwashed young supporters have caused a drop in Biden's poll numbers as he seeks re-election. What else would you expect when you have both students and faculty at Harvard (including ethnic Jews!) expressing their "understanding" of Hamas fighters and their motivation.

This self-defeating woke culture is omnipresent in the West right now, particularly in the US. It is obsessed with guilt over actions taken over the centuries against the downtrodden and subjugated masses of the global south; it is a virus spreading from university departments to the American student body. In this particular culture, every sadistic Hamas butcher is a progressive with the right to commit any atrocity against an age-old oppressor.

Biden is more focused on his re-election campaign than on the outcome of this global war. He has been forced to kowtow to the progressives and make concessions to them. But this will not help. He has already lost the election. And now he is somehow managing to lose a global war that the US looked certain to win.

These progressives despise the West and yearn for its defeat in both Ukraine and Israel. Their demands have been both logical and consistent—a permanent cease fire on both fronts of the global war. And they have help; the so-called "upscale" media in the US is under their thumb and are trumpeting this same line. But events have unfolded in such a way that a ceasefire would result in only one thing: Ukraine and Israel would surrender to enemies that are committed to their complete annihilation.

It would seem that Biden understands this perfectly well:

"Hamas and Putin represent different threats, but they share this in common: They both want to completely annihilate a neighboring democracy—completely annihilate it. Hamas—its stated purpose for existing is the destruction of the Jewish state. Meanwhile, Putin denies Ukraine has, or ever had, real statehood."

And yet this same Biden, time and time again, obediently joins the progressive chorus as it whines in unison: "Anything *but war*! We must do all we can to keep this conflict from escalating into a regional war."

The whole world is witnessing two fascist regimes trying to annihilate two heroic nations. These nations are fighting not only for their very existence but for the future of the Free World as well. It's hypocritical to call for a de-escalation. A de-escalation would mean surrendering to war criminals.

No, my friends—anything *but peace*. The US must insist on an escalation. But an escalation that would result in many fewer deaths than we are seeing now on a daily basis.

On the Ukrainian front. The West needs to tap into NATO's immense stores of high-precision weaponry—aircraft, drones, long-range missiles, anti-aircraft defense systems, tanks—and immediately ship it to Ukraine in amounts necessary for a victory (that is to say, driving out the occupiers from Ukrainian territory). The Ukrainian military will then gladly complete the rest of the mission on its own.

On the Israeli front. As far as I know America does still exist, so, then it should be in full accordance with Blinken's promise in Jerusalem: "We will always be there by your side." Although Hezbollah is preparing for a major attack on Israel, it is for now hesitant to carry it out. Now is the time for American carrier forces and the Israeli air force to order a series of strikes that will reduce Hezbollah to ashes. Its military infrastructure must be destroyed and the leadership's stylish mansions in Beirut totally obliterated. This would be a just act of vengeance taken against Hezbollah terrorists for crimes committed and yet to be committed and would be of political and military significance as well. But besides all that, it is an essential preliminary condition for the allies to carry out its Main operation—an airstrike on Iran, where the call for genocide of the Jewish people originated and is most actively promulgated. Iran makes no secret that the massive arsenal of missiles it has provided Hezbollah—and that is aimed at Israel—serves in part as a deterrent to the Jewish state, keeping it from striking Iran's nuclear capabilities.

There is a remarkable 28-page document on the House of Representatives website entitled "Proposed Plan for Victory in Ukraine." This plan is the work of three key House committees (Foreign Affairs, Armed Services, and Intelligence) and was introduced by their respective chairs—all Republicans (Michael McCaul, Mike Rogers, and Mike Turner).

I agree with every word of this document; I must admit that I have been saying exactly the same thing every day since the invasion took place two years ago, either on Ukrainian television or online on kasparov.ru.

All in all, the fact that this Plan exists and that it was presented at such a high level of government is an extremely positive thing; it shows, in my opinion, that the Reagan wing of the Republican party will play a decisive role in the election campaign. A possible talking point: Biden and other Democratic candidates are unwilling/unable/reluctant to pursue Victory in an existential war unleashed on the Free World by an Unholy Alliance of tyrants and murderers.

It is also significant that we now have a Republican candidate who is committed to Victory over the forces of Absolute Evil.

Rishi Sunak and Nimrata Randhawa, children of the Great Civilization of India, have been chosen by the Mahatma to lead the Free World at a critical moment in history, a moment when this world looked to be on the verge of collapse, with barbarians at the gate and traitors and hacks all around. Forty years have passed and the Anglo Saxons have proven incapable of producing an updated version of that 20th century duo for the ages—Ronald Reagan and Margaret Thatcher.

The Manchurian Candidate

First published on January 22nd, 2024

I

If Trump wins, he will enter the White House on January 21st, 2025 as a much more dangerous president than he was in 2017. He will be bitter and seek to take his revenge on the deep state that stole the election from him in 2020. Trump will also go after European leaders who he feels slighted him or looked down on him throughout his first term. Ukraine, which caused his first impeachment, will suffer, as well. If fact, it already has—an aid package has been held up for more than three months thanks to a handful of Trump's most rabid supporters in the House. They are even threatening to remove the Speaker if he dares to even put it up for a vote.

The US, Europe, and Ukraine: this is the same list of enemies compiled by Trump's long-time partner Vladimir Putin. These nations are also the recipients of his seething hatred. And so there they stand, gleefully winking at each other across the sea. They no longer need covert intermediaries or secret agreements. They know perfectly well as it is just what actions this tandem will take in the third week of January 2025.

Candidate Trump promises almost every day that he will stop the war in Ukraine within twelve hours of assuming the presidency, which is code for putting an end to US arms shipments.

And in the first twelve days, he says, he will meet and even surpass Putin's December 2021 ultimatum to NATO (which Putin himself no longer dares mention after his defeat at Hostomel in February 2022): "Pack up your shit and hightail it back to the Baty-Dzhugashvili line from 1245/1945."

Starting on the morning of January 22, 2025, a series of at first seemingly insignificant events will take place in several Central European nations. Then things will become more and more alarming. In Riga we will start to see aggressive marches of the dashing "veterans of the Great Fatherland War." In Narva, little green men will begin coming out of the woodwork, desecrating anything to do with the Estonian state. There will be a series of incidents on the Russo-Finnish border and around the Suwałki Gap. A pro-Russia demonstrator in Tallinn will be killed in a confrontation with police. Moscow will then issue stern warnings to a half a dozen NATO members, accusing them of Russophobia and of allowing a resurgence of Nazism on their soil. Meanwhile, Dmitriy Medvedev, the Chairman of the Security Council, will propose that Russia immediately launch precision nuclear strikes.

All eyes will naturally turn to Washington and Brussels. Trump will pause theatrically and offer no comment on the events. NATO headquarters, inundated with appeals from member states to invoke Article 4 and 5 of the NATO charter will be unable to stake out a position because one of the leading members of the alliance, the US, will not take part in discussions.

By the evening of January 25, Hungary, Slovakia, and Bulgaria will announce that they are withdrawing from NATO. And then on the 26th of January, US President Donald Trump will appear on television screens throughout the world to inform us that he is heading to Moscow first thing on the invitation of his friend Vladimir. There they will cut a terrific deal to ensure peace and security in Europe for decades to come. "You're going to love it," he'll tell the nations that have pressed NATO to enforce the security guarantees promised to them.

Putin will meet Trump in person at the airport and depart for the Kremlin in the same limousine, not wasting a moment in hammering out the details of this historic deal.

After a productive night hard at work with Putin, Trump will return to Washington. He will descend the stairs of Air Force One to greet his wellwishers, one hand raised triumphantly and clutching several sheets of paper.

He will reveal the contents of these documents several hours later in an address to the nation:

"My fellow Americans, my friend and crucial geopolitical partner, Vladimir, and I have come to the conclusion that an organization such as NATO, founded in the middle of the last century, is no longer up to the task of maintaining security in Europe. The fact that it keeps expanding, almost automatically, has already led to one major war on the continent. The organization is inherently resistant to reform. And so, we have decided we need new entities to provide security guarantees in Europe, namely the two Great Powers of the United States and Russia. Our first step will be to put an immediate end to the war in Ukraine. I have already issued an order to cease all arms shipments to the country. I will introduce a bill to Congress which officially recognizes the territorial integrity of Russian and Ukrainian borders as they are stipulated in the constitution of the Russian Federation. For his part, Vladimir is willing to recognize any government in Ukraine which 1) returns any Russian territory it is currently occupying and 2) is prepared to sign a Friendship and Good-Neighborliness Treaty with the Russian Federation, a treaty that will guarantee the rights of Russian speakers on Ukrainian territory.

"Vladimir intends to propose similar binding treaties to the governments of Latvia, Lithuania, and Estonia. If they give their consent, he will limit himself to a small number of territorial demands, that is to say those that are absolutely essential in ensuring Russia's security: returning the Narva area to Russia and turning over the Suwałki Gap to the Union State of Russia and Belarus, thus connecting it with the Russian territory of Kaliningrad."

II

There is even a possibility—a remote one, perhaps—that the West might lose a World War foisted upon it by the forces of absolute evil, despite its vastly superior military capabilities. The only thing that prevented the Ukrainian armed forces from achieving victory back in the fall of 2022 was a lack of political will on the part of the Americans. After many a protracted delay, the Ukrainians have finally received what I would call a rather limited array of Western weaponry. If they had had these weapons at their disposal during the attacks on Kherson and Kharkiv, Russian forces would have been soundly defeated.

There are two ways to avoid the catastrophic scenario I have outlined above. The first and more radical path is to achieve total victory over Putin's Russia well before January 21, 2025, ideally before the Republican and Democratic Conventions (slated for June and August 2024, respectively).

For this to work, the West must immediately deliver to Ukraine two hundred F-16s and the same number of ATACMS with a range of 200 miles. That way there will be no need for trench warfare or front-line breaches. Ukraine will simply annihilate the adversary's Crimea command at a remove, which will prove to be not only a military defeat, but a psychological and political catastrophe for the Putin regime.

III

The second method does not run counter to the first; on the contrary, it serves as its logical complement. It entails providing the American public with the opportunity to choose the most electable Presidential candidate. Of the three remaining candidates in the race, this person, in my opinion, is most certainly Nikki Haley. There is no way that either Donald Trump or Joe Biden can win—their approval numbers are too low. All the polling data show both Trump and Haley defeating Biden in a general election, but Haley wins by a larger margin.

Still not convinced? Then let's conduct a little experiment, one that our narrow-minded American pollsters have yet to bother with. Let's poll the widest selection of the American public and ask them one simple question: "Who would get your vote for President of the United States—Nikki Haley or Donald Trump?"

My working hypothesis goes like this: Nikki Haley would consistently come out on top of any such poll and is, therefore, the most popular choice for President among the American electorate. Then how is it that she might lose the Republican primary to Trump? For one simple reason—primary voters are not reflective of the United States or even of the Republican party as a whole. They represent the most partisan activists within the Republican party. The most qualified and electable candidate is often unable to make it through this internal party filtration system—a major flaw of the traditional American electoral system. But in this particular case, let's try to rectify that injustice.

First of all, the very act of conducting the experiment I proposed will bring many Americans to their senses and have a positive impact on Nikki Haley's chances to win the Republican nomination. And the foreign policy establishment wing of the Republican party (McConnell, Graham, McCaul, Roger, Turner) will then have to embrace the task facing the entire nation: making sure the Manchurian candidate does not enter the White House.

The Macron Doctrine

First published on March 19th, 2024, with Jason Galie

On March 7th, Joseph Biden, the President of the United States and supposedly the leader of the Free World, began his State of the Union address to Congress by touching on the most important issue of them all—Ukraine. He stated that this heroic and embattled nation was in dire need of financial and military assistance in its lonely struggle to defend this free world from the Rashist horde. He correctly compared Putin to Hitler and then pivoted to remind the audience of his esteemed predecessors who had delivered speeches in the very same room: Franklin D. Roosevelt, who defeated Nazism in Germany, and Ronald Reagan, who crushed that other Evil Empire—Soviet communism.

Biden spoke with utter sincerity, but no one seemed to believe him—not in Ukraine, in Russia, or in Europe. His admirable words seemed to have no effect. He had made almost the same statement five months ago in an address to the nation after Russia's ally Iran and its proxy terrorists attacked Israel. Biden at that time turned his words into deeds by submitting legislation to Congress, asking it to allocate 60 billion dollars of military aid to Ukraine.

But over the course of those five months we witnessed Donald Trump, a traitor to his country and a sworn enemy of the free world, threaten and blackmail Republicans into blocking the legislation from coming to the floor, eventually even getting them to withdraw their compromise bill on military aid and the southern border. In his rush to please Putin, Trump is no longer trying to hide his desire to extinguish Ukraine's fighting spirit.

Biden is responsible not only for failing to push that bill through Congress. For the first two years of the war, when the totalitarian sect gunning for the second coming of Trump had yet to cow a majority of Republicans into submission (at the time they were still fully in favor of aid to Ukraine), the Biden administration decided to play it safe and took much too long in approving each successive request for essential military shipments.

It seems the US simply doesn't have the will, and now it looks as though another great power might step up to the plate.

Trump's success in blocking military aid to Ukraine and the increasing possibility that he might return to the Oval Office have truly rattled European leaders. They have looked on helplessly as the basic foundations of peace on the continent, unshakeable for seventy-five years, have begun to crumble. For decades, these Europeans sat in their cozy cafes, safely protected by NATO Article 5, engaged in wholly unproductive discussions on the establishment of a European army. Eventually they looked over their shoulder and realized the only existing European army at the moment was the heroic Armed Forces of Ukraine—hardened in vicious battle as they kept the Asiatic horde from reaching Europe once again.

"Guaranteeing the security of Europe today requires more than merely rendering aid to this army—we must become an organic component of it. We must supplement it with the most advanced military equipment." French president Emmanuel Macron was the first to articulate this in a clear, persuasive manner, and in the language of Descartes and Pascal to boot. His recent statements directed at Moscow have been defiant and challenging.

We find ourselves today in another 1938 situation and we simply must end up on the right side of History. France is doing all it can to Defeat Russia in this war. The aggressor must vacate all Ukrainian territory that it has occupied since 2014. If need be, France and some of its allies are also willing to send their troops to Ukraine. French (and British) military experts are already deployed there to maintain the "Storm Shadow" and "Scalp" missile systems that we installed.

In any case, we have no intention of declaring any self-imposed red lines or any restrictions on the kind or number of weapons we can send to Ukraine. And we will be the ones to decide the number of service personnel to be deployed to maintain these systems (air defense system operators, air force pilots, electronic warfare specialists, etc.).

It's been a long time since someone talked to those Petersburg gangsters the way Macron did. But that's how they needed to be dealt with from the very beginning. The course of this World War, even history itself, seems to be pushing a new figure to the forefront, someone to assume the unfortunately vacant role of Leader of the Free World.

The heads of the Kremlin organized crime syndicate, blindsided by all this, responded with a reflexive boast about their Sarmats and their Poseidons. But Macron did not take the bait from these amateurs and simply added, "France also has nuclear weapons." And the discussion was over.

"How is it that we aren't responding to this outrageous rhetoric from Macron? Why aren't we bombing France, striking them hard with at least our world-class conventional weapons?"-so goes the almost hysterical response from Russian patriotic Z-thugs on all the Youtube and Telegram channels over the past few days.

The answer to those questions is simple: in such a scenario, the retaliatory long-range missile strikes from the combined air power of France, the UK, Sweden, Poland, Finland and possibly other NATO members would hit targets not only in Ukraine but deep within Russia as well. And no one will ask Grandpa Biden for permission. Europe might not have infantry divisions at the moment capable of relieving the Ukrainians on the front lines, but it has more than enough fire power to conduct strikes on Russia. The European Army should ensure Russia's defeat by January 21, 2025.

And what else do the Kremlin gangsters have to counter this Macron Doctrine? The Patrushev Ryazan Doctrine, naturally.

More than likely, the Russian intelligence services will move quickly to activate the "Islamic terrorist" sleeper cells they control in France. We will hear about them shortly.

As for Russia itself, if we are to believe the chorus of panicked Western diplomats in Moscow, Platonich (Patrushev) has already scattered the powder around and several "Ryazan" scenarios will unfold in the coming weeks. The first pilot group of "Islamic terrorists" were dealt with the other day in Kaluga oblast. The cover story was that they were about to attack a synagogue (of course) in Moscow. The objective behind these run-of-the-mill provocations is to provide justification for instating martial law and beginning a large-scale mobilization. The regime will then conduct a purge of those against the war along with anyone who dares to ask any uncomfortable questions. The Z-thugs might actually be first in line.

La Grandeur de la France

First published on April 1st, 2024, with Jason Galie

For the eight decades following the end of World War II, French diplomacy has sought to strike an enduring balance between solidarity with a NATO alliance that guaranteed security of the country, and a certain distancing from the US that demonstrated to the world at large, and to itself, la Grandeur de la France.

The nation's friends and allies have traditionally regarded this altogether French style of foreign policy with understanding coupled with a certain amount of irony.

But surely no one could have predicted during those 80 years that there would come a time in world history when a very real "la Grandeur de la France" would not only become necessary, but whose existence or absence might shape the fate of mankind.

The enemies of Freedom and the forces of absolute evil were quite deliberate when they chose their moments to attack Ukraine and Israel. Their objectives—the destruction of both nations—have never been a secret. They followed domestic US political events with close attention and witnessed two cancerous tumors develop and metastasize—one from the right (Trumpism) and one from the left (the Progressives). These tumors have eaten away at the traditional center within US politics and undermined the country's ability to fulfill its role as Leader of the Free World.

As we all know, Russia has faltered and fallen twice before in a matter of days, during both Tsarist and Soviet times. But what about the US? President Joe Biden has always considered himself, at least on a rhetorical level, the Leader of the Free World (a title neither Barack Obama nor Donald Trump claimed). But during his three years in office the world has watched him falter and fall completely in fulfilling this role, leaving behind a major hole in the system for international security.

The Trumpists in Congress have held up aid to Ukraine for almost six months. Chances are high that a fanboy of Russian President Vladimir Putin will soon occupy the Oval Office. And this particular fanboy will not hide his disdain for both Ukraine and US allies in Europe.

As 1938 dawned yet again with its gloom and its dread, this time for an embattled Ukraine and those who considered themselves part of the Free World, a glimmer of hope appeared on the horizon. French President Emmanuel Macron took stock of the unprecedented threat looming over the nation and presented a series of crucial propositions to the world at large. In our last article, we categorized these propositions as the Macron Doctrine:

- France will do all in its power to defeat Russia in its war with Ukraine
- France and some of its allies are willing to send troops to Ukraine
- French (and British) military experts are already in Ukraine servicing and maintaining the "Storm Shadow" and "Scalp" missile systems
- France has no intention of further aiding the enemy by imposing any kind of red lines on itself which might restrict support for an embattled Ukraine
- The dictator is trying to intimidate France with threats of nuclear strikes. To that I say, France also has nuclear weapons.

Macron was thus able to strike a serious psychological and political blow on Putin without yet deploying a single French soldier or delivering a single French aircraft to Ukraine. He deprived the aggressor of his most effective tool in his illicit war—the ability to suppress the West's political will by forcing it to establish these notorious red lines.

Macron's rhetoric stands out all the more when compared with the US national security advisor's visit to Kyiv which took place at roughly the same time.

Jake Sullivan arrived at an extremely difficult time for Ukraine, deprived as it was of US military aid. And then he had the gall to make an outrageous demand of the Ukrainians—stop striking Russian oil refineries. Yes, Grandpa Biden's advisor was actually advocating for more fuel so that Russian aircraft could continue to rain death upon Ukrainian cities. Why? Because this is what Grandpa needs for his re-election campaign.

But let's get back to the Macron Doctrine. How valuable a political victory this proves to be can best be measured using one criterion—the potential for it to achieve victory on the battlefield. In this specific case, how possible it is for Macron's announced objectives to result in defeat for Russia. We do not have a contact inside the French General Staff but we can share our view on how this goal can be reached.

How the Macron Doctrine could lead to Russian defeat

Let's start with a few observations concerning the fundamental nature of the Russia-Ukraine war. What we have are two different wars overlapping one other. The first one is a classic war of attrition waged on a nearly 1,000-kilometer line of contact between the two sides. In this war, Russia theoretically has the advantage thanks to a larger mobilization base and the traditionally low value Russian society places on an individual human life.

But the Russian military machine has one acute vulnerability—the Crimean peninsula. The clash over Crimea represents, as 19th century Prussian General Carl von Clausewitz would put it, the psychological center of gravity in the whole Russia-Ukraine war. And here, in this second component of the war, Ukraine clearly has the upper hand. The nation was able, without a navy to speak of or a modern air force, to toss Russia's Black Sea Fleet right out of Sevastopol and continues to eliminate Russian military facilities throughout the peninsula.

The five points contained within the Macron Doctrine, outlined above, are quite interrelated. Taken together, they provide the following scenario for a decisive defeat of the Russian Federation.

The Coalition of the Willing (France, Great Britain, Sweden, Poland, Finland, Romania, Canada, the Netherlands) will refuse to adhere to any ridiculous red lines imposed on them at US insistence, particularly a requirement that all Western aircraft supplied to Ukraine be flown only by pilots with Ukrainian passports.

This requirement has been truly ruinous for Ukraine as it has already prolonged a devastating war for at least a year. If Ukraine were to keep blindly adhering to it, the best-case scenario would be receipt of 30-40 different airplanes with 30-40 different specifications—not exactly the game changer needed to win a war. What Ukraine really needs to turn the tide in its favor are 150-200 aircraft comprising entire squadrons of Mirages from France, Typhoons from the UK, Gripens from Sweden.

These aircraft are able to integrate the "Storm Shadow" and "Scalp" systems much more efficiently and no restrictions should be placed on their range.

That's how we envision the Macron Doctrine being put into practice. The air armada would immediately instate a de facto no-fly zone over Ukraine and then quickly drive out the entire Russian alignment of forces from Crimea. The Ukrainian flag flying over Sevastopol would then signify Russia's defeat along with the death, at least political, of the bloodsucker in the Kremlin.

When the French and the British took Sevastopol on September 9, 1855, that Crimean War ended in precisely the same way. It's just that Nicholas I, the tsar who initiated the conflict, had had the sense to die six months earlier.

The Leaders of the Free World

First published on April 10th, 2024, with Jason Galie

Vladimir Putin and Donald Trump meet at the 2017 G-20 Hamburg Summit.[4]

These poignant photographs will preserve for posterity two fateful moments in the history of the 21st century. During a session of geopolitical wizardry, the triumphant Chekist trickster is able to eliminate, one after the other, the last two Emperors of modern-day Rome. The whole world watched first in Helsinki in 2018 and then in Geneva in 2021 as two different statesmen took the stage—it was the same diminutive, little man next to two notice-ably taller gentlemen. As soon as the figures appeared in front of the cameras, every single television viewer, and there were tens of millions watching, knew exactly which of them was the alpha male and which one was displaying a deep psychological dependency on his partner.

---

4   This photo is licensed under the Creative Commons Attribution 4.0 License; the source
     is http://kremlin.ru/events/president/news/55006/photos.

For the entire second half of the 20th century, the Oval Office was occupied by someone whom the world at large viewed as the leader of the West and of the Free World. But this symbolic chair has been empty for more than twelve years. Neither President Obama nor President Trump viewed himself as the leader of the West or of the Free World. Both men were keen to remove the United States from leadership roles on the global stage. The lefty Obama learned at his mother's knee that the United States had wronged "the oppressed peoples of the world" and would go on to apologize whenever he could for the "crimes committed" by "American imperialism" against the Arab world, the Vietnamese, and so on down the list. Trump was the complete opposite; his extreme right-wing stance held the entire world at fault for the US's woes, especially its Western allies that were always "hounding the US for money."

It was truly music to the Kremlin's ears when Trump slammed NATO and Article 5 of its Charter. It seems the Old Mole of History chose these two starkly different characters to solidify the US's retreat from the trends of world history.

US President Joe Biden (L) meets with Russian President Vladimir Putin (R) at the 'Villa la Grange' in Geneva on June 16, 2021.[5]

---

5   Photo by Mikhail Metzel via Getty Images; used with permission.

The Biden tenure

The rhetoric throughout Biden's election campaign and into the first months of his presidency focused on making up for this 12-year absence: "I'm back! The US is back in business!"

Here was someone who truly saw himself as the leader of the West and of the Free World. Biden spoke movingly about this at a Town Hall on July 21, 2021, not without a touch of vanity after his summit with Putin.

"It's the first time I ever felt like—you always hear people say 'leader of the free world.' Well, I realize, when I'm sitting across from Putin, who I know, he knows who I am; I know who he is. He knows I mean what I say and can do what I say. He understands. And we must be the leader of the free world. If we don't do it, nobody good is likely to do it or has the capacity to do it. I really mean it. I genuinely mean it." He seems honestly overwhelmed by the heady sensation he first felt in Geneva: "I am the leader of the free world. I'm sitting across from Putin and he knows I mean what I say and can do what I say. He understands."

Yes, the derisive expression on Putin's face after their meeting confirmed that he certainly did understand who Mr. Biden is and what he can do. In particular, he knew that half an hour later Biden would call a press-conference and robotically repeat a talking point crucial for Putin—that the Minsk Agreements alone represent the path forward. What's even more important—Putin realized that he "got exactly what he wanted from Biden in Geneva."

The majority of the US commentariat was in agreement with this—Biden had bombed his first audition for the role of leader of the Free World after telling us all how much he wanted it.

In Geneva, Putin sized up this so-called leader of the Free World and found him wanting. It was then that he made his final decision on how to tackle the issue of Ukraine.

Three years have passed from that moment. Hundreds of thousands of people have lost their lives in the bloodiest conflict on the European continent since 1945. Biden occasionally manages to say the right words (with the help of a teleprompter or a stack of index cards). Here he is addressing the nation in October 2023:

"Hamas and Putin represent different threats, but they share this in common: They both want to completely annihilate a neighboring democracy—completely annihilate it. If we don't stop Putin's appetite for power and control in Ukraine, he won't limit himself just to Ukraine."

But the Ukrainian military aid bill has languished in the House of Representatives for over a year and a half, blocked by Republicans on Trump's insistence. And as Ukrainian soldiers shed their blood on the field of battle, the Biden administration decided to send one of its top officials to Kyiv... to forbid Ukraine from striking Russian oil refineries with its UAVs.

So, more hellfire and more fuel for the Russian military machine that is "completely annihilating" Ukraine. Why? Because Grandpa Biden has his re-election campaign to think about—higher gas prices come November would not be good.

What must be done

The US political class as a whole has proven that the country is simply not capable of assuming the role of Leader of the Free World during a global war unleashed on Western civilization by the forces of absolute evil.

This war cannot be won by drawing red lines in the sand with unsteady hands, lines that do nothing except tie those hands behind our backs. Emmanuel Macron declared that we should refrain from imposing these much-ballyhooed restrictions. He agrees with Biden that "Putin won't limit himself to Ukraine." That is why, according to Macron, the West (the Coalition of the Willing) must defeat Russia in Ukraine standing side by side with the heroic Ukrainian army, the only force at the moment fulfilling the mission set forth seventy-five years ago in the founding documents of NATO.

The President of France made sure to point out that French service-members were already participating in military operations in Ukraine (helping to operate SCALP missiles). And in response to Putin's expected saber-rattling about nuclear strikes, Macron told the war criminal simply: "France has nuclear weapons, too."

Acting like that, France put in a serious bid for the position of Leader of the Free World, left vacant at a crucial moment in history.

A Renewed Entente Cordiale

Macron has made a brilliant strategic move by offering to share the burden of leadership of the Free World with the United Kingdom. The Foreign Ministers of the UK and France have made a politically game-changing joint declaration:

> "We are both absolutely clear: Ukraine must win this war. If Ukraine loses, we all lose. The costs of failing to support Ukraine now will be far greater than the costs of repelling Putin.
>
> "Britain and France are proud of the support we have provided to Ukraine, from unprecedented sanctions to coordinated deliveries of the first long-range missile systems, SCALP and Storm Shadow. Just last month, the first Ukrainian pilots graduated from training with the Royal Air Force to start training with the Armée de l'air et de l'espace, as part of a program to build up Ukraine's ability to fly modern F-16 fighter jets.
>
> "But we must do even more to ensure we defeat Russia. The world is watching—and will judge us if we fail."

Glory to Ukraine! Glory to a Renewed Entente!

A Rivalry for Leadership

First published on April 28th, 2024

On February 13, one of the toughest days for Ukraine in Washington, DC, I made note of the following:

> I am most interested in the stances of three prominent members of the Republican party—Michael McCaul, Mike Rogers, and Mike Turner. Each of them chairs a powerful house committee: Foreign Affairs, Defense, and Intelligence, respectively.
>
> The authors of the outstanding document Proposed Plan for Victory in Ukraine cannot possibly vote against military aid to Ukraine; this would mean renouncing their convictions on camera in front of the entire world. For that very reason I believe the Ukraine aid package will eventually be passed by the US Congress.

And that is exactly what has happened. McCaul, Rogers, and Turner all worked publicly and behind the scenes to score an ideological win for the Reagan wing of the Republican party over the pro-Putin, pro-Trump rabble in the House. They made good use of a classified Kremlin document published by Catherine Belton that describes Russia's methods to subvert Western support for Ukraine and accused their colleagues in the House of falling for Russian propaganda.

"It's absolutely true that some Republican members of Congress were repeating Russian propaganda about the invasion of Ukraine instigated by Russian President Vladimir Putin.

"Russian propaganda had infected a good chunk of our party's base.

Donald Trump and Volodymyr Zelensky met in New York as the Ukrainian tried to hedge Kyiv's position after disappointing meetings with the Biden administration.

"We see directly coming from Russia attempts to mask communications that are anti-Ukraine and pro-Russia messages—some of which we even hear being uttered on the House floor."

The Chair of the House Intelligence Committee did not name names, but the scoundrels in the chamber got the message; the vast majority wisely shut their mouths. Even the group's godfather, never at a loss for words, had nothing to say before the vote as he sat in court with his defense lawyers. Only the delusionally stupid Trumper Marjorie Taylor Greene continued to rant and rave.

The two parties that remain in the US are: the Capitulation Party (the progressives and the Trumpers) and the Victory Party (the Reagan wing of the Republican Party and the Truman wing of the Democratic one).

The day of the vote—April 20—resulted in a triumph for American-Ukrainian solidarity. One after another, lawmakers (both Republican and Democrat) came to the floor with comments that were spot-on; the same comments, by the way, that yours truly has been directing at them as best I could for almost 10 years; to wit:

1. The Russo-Ukrainian war is but one critical battlefield within a global war unleashed by the forces of Absolute Evil on the Free World with the goal to annihilate it;
2. 30 million Ukrainian Spartans have borne the brunt of this horrendous war for over two years now, literally using their bodies to protect the prosperous golden billion from the barbarians at the gate;
3. Delivering a large package of military aid to Ukraine is not only in the best interests of the United States from a security standpoint but also constitutes a debt of honor from a nation that still considers itself the Leader of the Free World.

We are witnessing a considerable restructuring of the American political space, which no longer has traditional Republican or Democratic parties.

As we approach a crucial, decisive moment in this global war, the two parties that remain in the US are: the Capitulation Party (the progressives and the Trumpers) and the Victory Party (the Reagan wing of the Republican Party and the Truman wing of the Democratic one).

It turns out a qualified majority (two-thirds of the votes) of both chambers is on the side of the Victory Party. You'd have to admit this is a curious turn of events. After all, the capitulators (of all stripes) had exerted their dominance for a shameful half of a year, blocking military aid to Ukraine or prohibiting it from conducting strikes on the aggressor's territory even with domestically produced weapons.

I do need to point out, however, that the size of the Ukraine aid package agreed upon is not enough to ensure victory. Don't get me wrong, it is absolutely needed at the moment. But it is also, in a way, a classic Biden aid package—simply enough to keep Ukraine from being defeated and to sustain its strategic defenses.

Nevertheless, I will still refer to the coalition that has materialized as the Victory Party. Its leaders, full of vigor and committed to the cause, have already proposed a Plan for Victory in Ukraine that sharply criticizes Biden for his insufficient support for the Ukraine.

In addition to the three chairmen factor that was in play, there is one other circumstance that favors a positive transformation of the American political arena. I am referring to Europe's reaction to the US's months of inaction. European leaders began to suspect that the US was either incapable or unwilling to fulfill its role as Leader of the Free World.

France and the UK (a Renewed Entente Cordiale) both declared their intention to defeat Russia in Ukraine and to refrain from drawing any sort of restrictive red lines when the West delivers military aid to the country. They also did not rule out putting troops on the ground in Ukraine and pointed out that French and British military specialists were already there to service the "Storm Shadow" and "SCALP" cruise missile systems the two nations had deployed.

What we are seeing emerge at this crucial moment in history is a healthy, productive rivalry between the US and Europe for the right to call itself the true Leader of the Free World. I wish both sides nothing but success in this most noble endeavor.

A Personal Duel: Macron vs. Putin

First published on May 11th, 2024

French President Emmanuel Macron is continuing his personal psychological duel against the dictator in the Kremlin, with vigor and resolve. If we recall, two and a half months ago, at an extremely difficult moment for Ukraine, he stated that defeating Russia in its war of aggression was an issue of his country's honor and security. He also did not rule out putting French troops on the ground in Ukraine.

When the Kremlin responded with the usual threats, including the expected saber-rattling about nuclear strikes, Macron issued two clarifications meant for the ears of one specific individual.

First of all, he felt it necessary to point out that "the French military is already taking part in combat activities on Ukrainian territory with their British counterparts. Their personnel are there to maintain the SCALP and Storm Shadow cruise missile systems that we delivered to the Ukrainians." Then he added dryly: "France has nuclear weapons, too."

Macron also stated: "It would be interpreted as weakness to establish a priori limits on ourselves when faced with such an adversary. What weakness!"

With these two statements, Macron not only dismantled the entire Kremlin propaganda machine designed for both domestic and international consumption, he also called into question the entire "strategic premise" of the war that Putin declared on the Free World.

Take a look at the type of discussions taking place on all the "patriotic" Russian TV channels at the moment. The Russian Z-lowlifes are yelling indignantly: "Macron has basically declared war on Russia. He's admitted that French soldiers are already taking part in combat activities. So why the hell haven't we conducted strikes on France? Okay, maybe we hold off on nuclear weapons, but we have amazing conventional arms that no one else in the world possesses."

The answer is simple: if Putin were to strike French territory, NATO's entire arsenal would come to bear on the Russian Federation. He would no longer be worried about the exact number, 40 or 60, of F-16 fighter jets the Dutch are going to ship to the Ukrainians. He would potentially be confronted with thousands of NATO aircraft.

Putin understands this perfectly. He has never had any intention of waging a conventional war with NATO. Or a nuclear one, for that matter. He took stock of all the Chamberlains in the West and figured he could get by with just the threat of nuclear strikes.

This all started when he annexed Crimea and stated: "Russian nuclear capabilities now stand at combat readiness in the event that Western nations engage us in a military standoff."

This also includes the "ultimatum" demanding that the West capitulate and move out of the Golden Horde's sphere of vital interests—from those of the Batu Khan in 1245 to Joseph Jughashvili's (aka Stalin) in 1945.

After Putin's Munich Security Conference speech in 2007, the world began to wonder just what methods Russia could use to engage in a successful confrontation with NATO, other than its famous "spirituality." After all, it lags far behind NATO nations in terms of economic development, science and technology, and conventional weapons.

Putin provided a clear answer in a joint press-conference with Macron on February 9, 2022—nuclear blackmail. The actual quote was:

> Of course, we can't compare Russia's conventional weapon arsenal to NATO's. We understand that. But we also understand that Russia is one of the world's leading nuclear powers. And when it comes to certain state-of-the-art components, we are ahead of many.

Here it seems Putin was taking the opportunity to remind his counterpart that as of February 2022, according to SIPRI statistics, Russia had 1,588 deployed strategic nuclear warheads while France had 280. But if Putin ever used this "we are ahead" stance to engage in a nuclear war with France, he would not be around long enough to enjoy the advantage. That 1,588th nuclear warhead would not be necessary. Russia and France would simply both cease to exist as modern states after the first 10 or so exchanges of nuclear strikes.

On February 26, 2024, Emmanuel Macron became the de-facto leader of the Free World. The traditional leader of record—the United States—is clearly no longer up to the task. The Trumpers in Congress held up the military aid package to Ukraine for more than four months, while the Biden administration itself struggled to articulate its goals in this war. At times it felt as if they were more apprehensive at the thought of Russia losing than of Ukraine being defeated.

In any case, the administration repeatedly imposed restrictions on itself with red line after red line. First it was: we don't dare provoke Putin; then it was: we have to prevent an escalation of the conflict, keep it from turning into a regional war.

In Macron's first speech in his new role, he sharply criticized the West's suicidal policy of red lines in a war with a fascist regime that establishes no red lines of any kind for itself.

In three and a half short months, Macron saw a great deal of success. He has powerful friends now who basically agreed with him in the West, namely the Reagan wing of the Republican party (Michael McCaul, Mike Rogers, and Mike Turner). This cohort, inspired (and in a way, left vulnerable) by Macron's new stance and role, managed to defeat the Trumpers in Congress and push through the Ukraine military aid bill.

Even more importantly, they became a vital component of an over-whelming, pro-Ukraine bipartisan majority (80 in the Senate and 322 in the House) that criticized Biden for insufficient military aid to Ukraine. The fact that Ukraine has now been granted long-range ATACMS (finally!) is a direct result of this pressure.

On April 7th (the 120th anniversary of the signing of the original Entente Cordiale), Great Britain and France announced the establishment of a Renewed Entente Cordiale. The parties decided to further cement the historic nature of this event by making a solemn promise to crush the aggressor: "We must do even more to ensure we defeat Russia. The world is watching—and will judge us if we fail."

And unlike their overly cautious American counterparts, Brits actually encourage and support strikes of their cruise missiles (550 km range) on any military target on Russian territory.

Now for the most important point. There are about 2,000 of the Russian President's top associates assembled in the Kremlin today for the coronation of Putin V. Total scoundrels every one of them, but still a rather well-informed lot. They are aware of everything I have outlined above. The dictator for life can see it in their eyes. They want to ask a question but can't: "We have lost the war, boss. How do we get ourselves out of this?"

They'll start talking eventually. In two months or so when the Mirages from France and the Typhoons from the UK, fitted with Storm Shadow and SCALP missiles, blow the symbol of Putin's misguided escapade to smithereens. I am referring to the Crimea bridge.

Putin's War Post-Patrushev

First published on May 15th, 2024

> "We cannot know further ways of our word—how
> it'll be drifted—Compassion from above is gifted as
> we are given sacred grace."
> –F. M. Tyutchev

On May 11th, the Kyiv Post published my opinion piece "A Personal Duel," addressing how the French President, Emmanuel Macron was able to instruct the West in two and a half months that it need not fear Putin's nuclear blackmail and it had to stop placing absurd limitations on itself with red lines.

My words (not mine, of course, but those of Macron) have drifted far and wide it seems.

On May 12th, Putin moved both his Minister of Defense, Sergei Shoigu, and his Secretary of the Security Council, Nikolai Patrushev sideways.

In my view Patrushev's removal and subsequent appointment to the seemingly humiliating post of Nautical Engineering Advisor, was the more significant of the two. He has been the main ideological force behind Russia's strategy of nuclear blackmail as an essential tool for the country in its war with the West. For a long time, this strategy worked, paralyzing any semblance of Western decisiveness.

But the West couldn't go on quivering in fear forever in the face of these two-bit Petersburg gangsters and their nuclear crowbar—first Ukraine, then the Baltics, and then where? The West was not going to simply disappear from the pages of history with a smile on its face like the Cheshire cat. At some point things had to change, although the US seems to have run out of any politicians with the cojones needed to stand up to Moscow.

It was left to the President of France to face up to his Russian counterpart using the type of language Putin would understand. And, for good measure, he did a little saber-rattling of his own by mentioning France's own 880 strategic nuclear warheads. In doing so, Macron effectively nullified Putin's nuclear threats, and naturally, put an end to Patrushev and his "strategic thinking."

It is telling how Kremlin propaganda has shifted its focus of late. Gone are the threats of nuclear apocalypse directed at France and the UK; now we hear only that their troops will perish on a massive scale on the conventional battlefields of Ukraine.

The abject failure of the nuclear blackmail strategy has deprived Putin of any chance of the victory that he and Patrushev envisioned: the complete destruction of the Ukrainian state. From this point on Putin will scramble to bring this conflict to some kind of a draw, one "honorable" enough that he is able to stay in power—by, for instance, securing some territorial gains.

In any case the fact that Russia has had to walk back some of its announced goals in this war, one of which was ordering NATO to "take your stuff and get the hell out of here," calls for a reckoning: several high-ranking officials should be declared guilty and punished.

The highly publicized arrest of Timur Ivanov, Shoigu's personal embezzler and Yuri Kuznetsov, the head of Russia's Defense Ministry personnel branch, demonstrates that Putin has already planned a "Grand Trial of thieves and traitors" within its Arbatskaya Square headquarters.

And now the "Honest Old Man" Belousov has been appointed as a civilian Minister of Defense. His role: to become appalled by and then reveal to the populace at large the horrific levels of thievery, decay, and betrayal by a significant number of generals. In such a way, Putin hopes to escape the blame for a war that has, for all intents and purposes, already been lost.

The Kremlin is now pushing two talking points for international consumption: "a long war" or a "Korea scenario." From the activity of Kremlin assets in Washington, that I have seen, this time Moscow would suggest a true Korea scenario, with no restrictions placed on Pyongyang's equivalent in "South" Ukraine, something different from the spring 2022 negotiations.

Russia would like to annex parts of Ukrainian territory while the rest of the country would remain an independent state free to ensure its security with both its own military capabilities and a military-political alliance of its choosing—whether it be NATO membership, an Entente Cordiale, or the EU.

The Kremlin hopes to use this "Korea scenario" to seduce that portion of Ukrainian society tired of the war and persuade the (current and future)

US administration's position that the only alternative to this scenario would be "a long war of attrition."

I am not sure just how long, but the Russians have at least another month and a half to conduct devastating strikes on Ukrainian cities and use their soldiers as cannon fodder to attack Ukrainian positions before some sort of balance is restored as Western aircraft arrive and more missiles and ammunition are delivered.

If the Russian-Ukrainian war had been really a war of attrition along a 1,000-kilometer line of contact, then we could have a conversation about a "Korea scenario." In fact this particular war has a different center of gravity (cf. Clausewitz)—the Crimean Peninsula, the most vulnerable area of the Russian military machine. Ukraine was able to boot the Russian navy out of Crimean ports with virtually no air force and no navy of its own.

What a betrayal, what a colossal mistake it would be to give up the Autonomous Republic of Crimea and its wonderful inhabitants to some Russian equivalent of North Korea. This is especially true if we consider that it would take only a small increase in logistical help for Kyiv, from a coalition of the willing, for Ukraine to conduct an audacious land, sea, air military operation to liberate Crimea. Then there would be no basis for a long war of attrition.

Pro-Ukrainian Shift in US Congress and Its Implications

First published on May 25th, 2024

The Reaganesque revolution that has taken place in Congress, forming a bipartisan pro-Ukraine majority, is gaining momentum. A vibrant, charismatic leader has come to the fore—the Chairman of the House Foreign Affairs Committee, Michael Thomas McCaul, Sr.

McCaul taught a masterclass in the House on May 22nd, pointing out on a map just what a betrayal it was to forbid Ukraine to use US weapons to strike targets in Russia.

This ban has always been unjust and mean-spirited towards a heroic ally of the US. McCaul made this clear, yelling to Secretary of State Antony Blinken as he tried to answer McCaul's questions: "It is now completely inconceivable!" He backed up his argument, stating: "We have Russian aircraft in Russian airspace over Belgorod using glide bombs to destroy entire city blocks in Kharkiv."

Blinken didn't even try to object. During a joint press-conference in Kyiv last week with Ukraine's Minister of Foreign Affairs, Dmytro Kuleba, Blinken finally agreed that it was completely up to Ukraine how it uses the weapons it receives to fight its mortal enemy.

Still, McCaul wouldn't let up: "Why the hell does [Jake] Sullivan and your administration continue to insist on this ban?" He made a point to call out by name his main opponent and Ukraine's enemy No. 1 in Washington.

The sleazebag had the nerve to show up in Kyiv at a time when it had no ammunition (thanks to the US) and demand that Ukraine stop using its drones to strike Russian oil refineries. A rise in oil prices, you see, might negatively impact Grandpa Biden's re-election campaign.

The Ukrainians responded unkindly to Sullivan. And McCaul's memorable performance in the House on May 22nd sends a clear message. Ukrainians can strike not only using British Storm Shadows and French Scalps, but American ATACMS as well. No one in Washington dares to speak out against the idea now.

I wrote in a previous column about the productive competition at play between Washington and Paris for the role of Leader of the Free World. A similar competition, no less fruitful, is underway within Washington for the very same mantle. (The next day, the hapless Blinken came under fire again from Senator Cruz for his insufficient support for Israel).

Putin is no Master of the Universe

Isolated from the world by his entourage, Joe Biden was the last person left who believed Russian President Vladimir Putin and his nuclear saber-rattling. Sullivan never believed him. It was his job to scare Biden with the prospect of a global nuclear war.

Perhaps more importantly, Putin himself no longer believes in his own nuclear blackmail. French President Emmanuel Macron has beaten him on a psychological level, while the three Republican musketeers in the House (McCaul, Rogers, Turner) deprived him of any last glimmer of hope for "victory" when they overcame the six-month, Trump-enforced, blockade on military aid to Ukraine.

Putin's rather calm and reasonable reaction to this tragic (for him) turn of events shows he is just a run-of-the-mill cynical gangster from St. Petersburg. He is not the Master of the Universe. So, he has turned to the existential task at hand—how to remain in power (and, consequently, survive) as his country suffers a defeat.

It seems the first practical steps he has taken in this new reality have been completely rational. He wants to postpone the defeat for as long as possible (the concept of a long war of attrition). He has placed the blame on the military exposing the widespread thievery present in the Ministry of Defense. He aims to neutralize any potential activists in the army. Yet Russia is now filled with NKVD agents, drunk on their own immunity from prosecution and general omnipotence, along with regional barons who now have their own gangster-filled private military companies.

The meltdown within Russian society has already begun and is impossible to stop. At the cost of massive human losses, Ukraine has prevented the spread of Rashist magma to the prosperous lands of Europe. The individuals and institutions so eagerly striving to become Leaders of the Free World can and should help Ukraine immediately as it tries to rid its sovereign territory of the toxic by-products of a complete collapse of Russian statehood.

This task could be fulfilled tomorrow, in two weeks, or in two months. It all depends on the West's political will. All the physical components necessary to complete it are present. The 200 NATO aircraft (French, British, Swedish) stationed on the airfields of Romania, Poland, Finland, and Ukraine could instate a no-fly zone over all of Ukrainian territory.

Threatened with the immediate destruction of its Crimean alignment of forces, Russian military leadership would then sign a memorandum stipulating the organized withdrawal of all Russian troops beyond the borders of Ukraine as they were in 1991.

My Theory for Delivering Victory to Ukraine

First published on June 2nd, 2024

An article appeared last week in the *Foreign Affairs* journal entitled "A Theory of Victory for Ukraine" which immediately sparked broad interest and comment across the globe.

The authors, Ukraine's former Minister of Defense, Andriy Zagorodnyuk, and Eliot A. Cohen, a well-known American diplomat and political scientist, rightly point out that until recently the US and the West as a whole refrained from using the term "victory" and generally avoided describing its goal in Ukraine as a Russian defeat, at least in public.

Washington has contented itself with the largely meaningless statement that it will support Ukraine "for as long as it takes," but the authors suggest that now "The West must explicitly state that its goal is a decisive Ukrainian victory and Russian defeat."

The authors are completely justified in chastising the West and their demand, especially concerning the US, is quite appropriate. However, to be fair, a growing number in the West are not only explicitly calling for the defeat of Russia once and for all but are also actively working to establish a "coalition of the willing" that would make that goal a reality.

I am referring first and foremost to the President of France, Emmanuel Macron, who rendered Putin's continuing nuclear saber-rattling completely ineffective by reminding the Kremlin that "France is also a nuclear power" as well as for renewing the "Entente Cordiale" by saying: "Britain and France are both absolutely clear: Ukraine must win this war. If Ukraine loses, we all lose. But we must do even more to ensure we defeat Russia. The world is watching—and will judge us if we fail."

Thanks to Michael McCaul's brilliant speech in the US Congress in his role as Chair of the Foreign Affairs Committee, the red line the traitor [CIA Director} Burns drew in the sand in private conversation with Putin in November 2021 has all but been eliminated. This line put in place the ban on using American weapons to strike Russian territory, which Secretary of State Blinken is now asking President Biden to lift.

It seems in principle the authors' appeal to the West to frame its political objective in the war as Russia's total defeat has been duly noted. Now all that needs to be done is to outline the sequence of steps the military needs to take on both the operational and strategic levels in order to achieve this goal.

The authors of the article describe the following possible sequence: the West increases regular shipments of ammunition, missiles, and air defense systems; the long-awaited F-16s finally arrive all of which effectively gives Ukraine all it needs to implement the authors' plan for a victory: "The process of softening Russian positions and weakening Russian resolve will likely take about a year, after which Ukraine should reclaim the initiative. Kyiv should again launch limited counteroffensives, which will allow it to retake key terrain."

Although I greatly respect the authors and stand in full solidarity with their political position, I believe what they have proposed is not so much a plan for Ukraine to win the war but rather a way to prolong it for several years with the sides butting heads up and down the well-fortified line of contact and the casualties mounting

I also have to differ with the authors' claim from the epigraph. Someone has come up with a theory. For three months now, in step with Macron's initiatives, the renewed Entente Cordiale, and the coalition of the willing, I have been developing my own Theory of Victory for Ukraine.

The war in Ukraine is not merely a stalemate confrontation along the thousand-kilometer line of contact. It has, in my opinion, a completely different center of gravity (cf. Clausewitz)—the Crimean Peninsula. Both sides in this war value the immense political symbolism Crimea represents.

At the same time, it represents the most vulnerable component of the Russian military machine. Ukraine managed to force Russian naval forces out of Crimean ports despite lacking its own aircraft or naval fleet. And now, having received long-range missiles, Ukraine has been striking airfields in the Crimea on a regular basis. It turns out Russian air defense systems there aren't up to the task.

If the skies over Ukraine become dotted with 100, or, even better, 200 state-of-the-art Western aircraft, the country will not only gain supremacy in the air, it will also render Russia's occupation of the Crimea untenable. It will have to withdraw from the peninsula or be completely destroyed remotely.

What's preventing the world from witnessing such a magnificent finale? One of those absurd, artificial red lines that Ukraine and its allies have imposed on themselves, this one stating only Ukrainian pilots can be at the controls of Western aircraft. We have been waiting for these pilots for two years. It's possible we will see a few dozen of them in the next two or three months. But no way will we get the necessary 100-200.

Ukrainian pilots flying F-16s over the skies of Ukraine is a good thing. A beautiful thing. But it's not a path to victory. A path to victory, a quick and decisive one, at that, would require cohesive combat units from the Air Forces of France, the UK, and Sweden deployed from the airfields of Romania, Poland, and Finland.

This is not just wishful thinking. It is a very real way to implement the top-notch conceptual framework proposed by Macron and the coalition of the willing that he has been assembling since February 26: "We must defeat Russia. I do not rule out putting French boots on the ground in Ukraine. Our military is already taking part in combat operations in Ukraine." France also has nuclear weapons. France intends to dispatch military instructors to Ukraine.

On June 6th, Macron will meet with Ukraine's Volodymyr Zelensky in Normandy to discuss what they should do together to defeat Russia—it seems obvious to me what must be done.

Post-Normandy Putler

First published on June 23rd, 2024

Western leaders gathered recently to mark the 80th anniversary of the Allied invasion of Normandy during World War II. The setting offered a poignant and historically mobilizing platform for these Allies who are currently involved in a Fourth World War being waged in both Europe and the Middle East. (The Third World War, the Cold War, was lost by the USSR and Putin has now unleashed a fourth. He wants to avenge this defeat the same way Hitler started World War II to avenge Germany's loss in World War I.)

"Putin is the Hitler of our day. Under no circumstances can we repeat the tragic mistake of the 1930s." These words, when spoken on the shores of Omaha Beach, sound all the more organic and persuasive.

This same motif dominated the discourse days later when world leaders met with the President of Ukraine in the Élysée Palace, at the G7 Summit in Italy, and at the Peace Summit in Switzerland.

The past three and a half months have seen a truly significant shift in the goals of Western leaders in the Russo-Ukrainian War. Two individuals played a key role in this process. On February 26, French President Emmanuel Macron announced, in the first of a series of statements on the war in Ukraine, that France and its closest allies intended to deliver a decisive defeat to the Russian Federation. In addition, he did not rule out putting French boots on the ground in Ukraine and sharply criticized the US's posture of self-imposed restrictions, or "red lines," when confronting the aggressor. When Putin responded immediately by trying to blackmail Macron with talk of nuclear strikes, Macron pointed out that French military specialists were already taking part in combat operations in Ukraine by maintaining the SCALP missile systems that France had supplied. He then offered Putin a rather modest reminder that France is also a nuclear power. The Z-patriots in Russia were not pleased the next morning when they realized no nuclear strike had been carried out on Paris. And with that, Putin's 15-year policy of nuclear saber-rattling ended with a whimper.

Across the pond in the United States, Michael McCaul, the charismatic Chair of the House Foreign Affairs Committee, led a revolution of the

Reagan wing of the Republican Party, a revolution that overcame months-long resistance from the Trump-backed lowlifes in Congress and resulted in the passing of a $61 billion military aid package to Ukraine. The timorous Biden administration was then forced to retract the most absurd and shameful of its "red lines."

And so now, as I see it, we have a certain "division of labor" at work among Ukraine's allies—the US and the "Coalition of the Willing" (France, the UK, Poland, Sweden, Finland, Romania, Estonia, Latvia, Lithuania, the Netherlands, Czechia, Canada, and Norway). Grandpa Biden will never retract the most serious of his red lines—to never send American troops to Ukraine. But the US will play another useful role—and this is something Europe is incapable of doing on its own—by supplying Ukraine with the necessary number of artillery rounds and missiles to conduct the daily exchange of strikes currently taking place along the line of contact between the two sides. Europe simply does not have the production capability for this. The US will thus guarantee an equilibrium akin to a stalemate along the thousand-kilometer frontline. Meanwhile, the Coalition of the Willing will take on the most interesting and inspiring component of the Victory plan located within the war's center of gravity (see Clausewitz)—the Crimean Peninsula. The Crimea is Russia's Achilles heel. The Armed Forces of Ukraine met quite a bit of success there even during the six-month period when ammunition was in short supply.

But can you imagine if 100-200 state-of-the-art Western fighter jets appeared on the scene, equipped with long-range missiles and controlled from an integrated central command center? They would also have access in real time to all information needed to strike potential targets. Ukraine has yet to receive these aircraft but Sweden, one of the more active members of the coalition, has already provided two of these flight centers. Sweden has returned to the world stage with gusto after a 200-year holiday. These centers will of course be outfitted with Swedish flight crews (five people).

Yet if the West is serious about defeating Russia by pursuing this most obvious scenario, it will have to reject the most absurd red line of all—the one that states only Ukrainian pilots can be at the controls of aircraft supplied to the country. There is a reason that Macron has emphasized so insistently of late—"I intend to send Ukraine Mirages, I intend to send Ukraine French military specialists." Here I translate from French to English—"I intend to send French air force detachments to Ukraine. They will be stationed at airfields in Romania and Poland along with British and Swedish air squadrons."

Now let us take a moment to look at the situation that has unfolded through the eyes of the architect of this Fourth World War. He must understand that his nuclear saber-rattling is no longer having the desired effect and that he is certain to lose a conventional war with the West. The role of Master of the Universe is out of reach, and he is now faced with a literally existential problem—how to remain in power (and, by extension, alive!) in a country that has just lost a war.

Yes, Putler understands he will never take Kyiv, or Odesa, or Kharkiv, but he is still holding out hope that will be able to reach a truce that he can sell to his people as a more or less honorable draw. He recently made a first attempt at selling this lie in an address to diplomats at the Ministry of Foreign Affairs. The speech was so underwhelming that he was likely unable to persuade even his own people in attendance. Their reaction to the speech was much more informative for me than the incoherent rambling of the orator as he read from his notes. For a moment I could not recall just where I had seen these very same faces in such a cavernous meeting hall.

I suggest you watch the video of the speech. There are many moments when the camera pans the audience. The sycophants all have the same stone-faced, dreary expression. They are all still loyal, it would seem, but clearly do not believe a word Putler is saying.

And then it hit me! We see the same thing in newsreels from Nazi Germany: Goebbels' speech to party activists in March 1945.

For Putler, the summer of 2024 will mark his spring of 1945.

Fake Shahed Putin Plays His Last Scoundrel Card— Trump

First published on June 30th, 2024

We are now in the third year of a full-blown Russo-Ukrainian war (the primary front of World War 4) and Putin has suffered a decisive defeat on the most crucial level of this global confrontation—the psychological. His most effective strategic tool over many years—nuclear blackmail—is no longer producing the desired results.

When the leader of a nuclear power threatens to use his country's nuclear weapons in pursuit of a localized geopolitical objective, there are two possible motives at play.

Number one—he is a suicide Shahed drone, actually willing to carry out a nuclear strike that kills millions of people. He is then also willing to die along with millions of his countrymen after the retaliatory strike is launched. (We will reach the pearly gates while they will simply drop dead).

The other motive—he is a calculating terrorist who realizes that the other side possesses a no less powerful arsenal of nuclear weapons. But he thinks this other side will blanch at the prospect of killing millions of people and make concessions within the framework of a discrete political conflict by meeting any demands put on the table. This will eventually result in the other side retreating from the world stage forever.

That exact scenario has played out over the past fifteen years or so. After Russian troops invaded Georgia, annexed Crimea, and then committed large-scale war crimes in Ukraine, the West placed artificial restrictions on the real military aid it was willing to provide in the form of cowardly red lines: "Under no circumstances must we allow this conflict to escalate and turn into a pan-European war. We must avoid confronting a nuclear power."

As winter came to a close in 2024, these were the sentiments that held sway in Washington. These sentiments, coupled with a months-long hold on US weapons shipments to Ukraine, almost resulted in the Rashists breaching the Ukrainian front. The strategic threat that this breach would have posed to the West as a whole forced the Free World to mobilize.

The world witnessed two conceptual revolutions unfold at once. President Macron of France led one in Europe while in the US, it was the leaders of the Reagan wing of the Republican party (McCaul, Rogers, Turner) who played the decisive role. Together they managed, in the spring of 2024, to fundamentally alter the political and psychological posture of the Free World's confrontation with Putin and his terrorists.

The West's present stance on the war is best reflected by the themes and statements expressed when Allied leaders met recently in Normandy: "Putin is the Hitler of our time."

The natural outgrowth of such a narrative is the West's determination to deliver a decisive defeat to Hitlerite Russia on the battlefield in Ukraine. For this to happen, the West needs to remove every restrictive red line it imposed on itself.

Remember, Putin became a laughing stock by relying too much on empty nuclear threats. As NATO Secretary General Stoltenberg stated a few days ago, "It seems every day Putin is blowing someone up with a nuclear weapon."

Macron made sure to remind Putin, however, that France is also a nuclear power. He also brightened the Russian leader's day by informing him that French service members are already taking part in combat activities in Ukraine by maintaining the SCALP missile systems that France provided.

The West pursued this line of thought by developing and promoting a transparent and convincing scenario for Ukraine to deliver a decisive defeat to the enemy's alignment of forces at the war's center of gravity (cf. Clausewitz)—the Crimean peninsula.

All this news has hit the Putin worshippers and fanatical Z-patriots like a ton of bricks in recent weeks. We have seen a new sentiment spread like a forest fire among this group of late—a sentiment that poses a great danger to Putin's political future—"The Tsar is not real!"

Putin is aware of this danger and will have to radically shift his goalposts. He no longer has the makings of Master of the Universe. He is faced now with an existential (in the most literal sense) problem—how to remain in power in a country that has just lost a war.

There is only one way to solve this problem and that is to prevent the fall of Crimea, a circumstance that would prove disastrous for Putin personally. He badly needs to retain significant parts of Ukrainian territory (including Crimea) for his Reich, something he will try to do via political machinations through his agents in the West. If successful, Putin would then be able to sell this outcome to his people as a kind of respectable draw, one achieved despite the rampant thievery and treason of many top generals.

But now, after Normandy, things have changed. There is not a single elected politician in the West willing to grant this dictator such a favor. And so we see him turning in desperation to play his final card: Donald Trump.

And then Trump pops up out of nowhere with his advisors' plan to end the war. What's more—he empathizes to such a degree with his embattled friend Vlad that he promises to enact his wonderful plan not on January 21, 2025, but, earlier, on November 5, 2024!

Trump has puzzled observers more than once with his Putinophilia, an affinity that does not seem to be backed by any rational motive. Perhaps the answer to the riddle lies in their notorious joint performance in Helsinki on July 16, 2018.

After a two-hour, one-on-one meeting, the two world leaders emerged, one sneering like the lowlife little thug that he is and the other, much taller, appearing somewhat groggy. Of the tens of millions of viewers watching from home, not a single one could have doubted which of the two was the alpha male and which was experiencing a deep psychological dependence on his counterpart.

P. S. Biden's disastrous performance at last night's debates probably sharply increased Trump's chances to return to the White House. That means only that The Deep Free World (led by Macron, McCall, Roger, Turner) should execute its Ukraine Victory scenario before November 5, 2024.

Overcoming the Dementia of the Free World

First published on July 13th, 2024

The debate on June 27th between the two candidates for US president—and, consequently, for the position of Leader of the Free World—provided definitive proof to all of us, supporters of this world, and, most importantly, to those fighting and dying now for the right of Ukraine to be free, that the United States is experiencing a profound political and moral crisis.

At a moment when the forces of absolute evil have challenged the very idea and existence of a Free World, the US political system has nominated two candidates to lead it: One is physically and mentally weak; an old man who throughout the four years of his presidency has carefully and cowardly portioned out military aid to Ukraine lest it might achieve—perish the thought—decisive victory over . . . the most insidious enemy of the US.

The other is an utter reprobate known for his "mysterious" psychological addiction to the dictator in the Kremlin. As the whole world looks on, he openly uses Viktor Orban as an intermediary to work with Putin on a joint plan to force Ukraine to surrender.

Such is the clinical diagnosis of the former Shining City on the Hill. If it does not undergo radical treatment soon, the global institution known for about a century as the Free World will find itself tossed unceremoniously into the dustbin of history on November 5, 2024.

But where can we find a collective healer capable of curing the American political system? In fact, one has already appeared on the scene, thankfully. I am referring to the bipartisan pro-Ukraine majority from both chambers of Congress that has emerged thanks to the conceptual revolution performed by the Reagan wing of the Republican party.

This majority overcame stubborn resistance from the Trumpers in Congress to pass a military aid package to Ukraine and forced the reluctant Biden administration to backtrack on several of its most repulsive "red lines" concerning this aid. The bill also included a demand that the administration articulate to Congress within forty-five days to Congress what it seeks to achieve in the Russo-Ukrainian war (the deadline passed).

The ideological leaders of the pro-Ukraine majority (McCaul, Rogers, and Turner) laid out their vision for what must be achieved in the war about eight months ago in a remarkable document—the "Proposed Plan for Victory in Ukraine." In it, the authors sharply criticize the Biden administration for not providing sufficient aid to the country.

The White House should be occupied by people willing and able to implement this "Proposed Plan," not those digging a grave for the Free World using a Putin/Trump/Orban plan to eliminate the Ukrainian state as a shovel.

Theoretically, there are two possible ways the current election cycle might enable this noble goal to be reached. The first might seem the most natural. Delegates at the Republican National Convention next week nominate one of two shining stars of their party for President—either Nikki Haley or Michael McCaul. Even better, they nominate them both as a package deal. They beat any candidate the Democrats put up in a landslide and then move to implement the "Proposed Plan" of their own creation.

Unfortunately, this scenario is not possible due to the rigid primary system of candidate nomination. Haley's path to the ballot is now closed, despite the fact she would have a better chance of winning the general election than Trump, who will be automatically nominated at the convention.

Thus, we are forced to go down a much more difficult path, approaching from the opposite wing of the political spectrum. Decrepit Biden will have to step aside as a candidate for President, ideally as soon as possible. The Democrats will determine their candidate. This new candidate's success will depend not so much on his/her personal biography or qualifications as much as on the strategy the democratic administration and campaign staff comes up with.

Technologically the best option for Democrats is Kamala Harris. One very simple reason. Because on account of his advanced age and worsening health, Biden may not only step aside as a candidate but logically resign the presidency as well.

Upgrading to the President level will dramatically expand the electoral opportunities of the former Vice-President Kamala Harris.

The main weakness of the current democratic strategy is its Trumpo-centricity: "Biden is old and senile, but only he can prevent Trump from returning to power!"

If such a lackluster and defensive campaign strategy is employed, any candidate will surely lose, no matter how many cognitive tests he manages to pass.

A fundamental change of campaign strategy is needed to go on the offensive with a positive, self-assured inspiring message.

On day one, President Harris should include the Republican "Proposed Plan" into her campaign platform as a key strategic element. In her response to Congress regarding the US's goals for the war in Ukraine she declares: "Russia's total defeat. Full restoration of Ukraine's territorial integrity. Russian war criminals brought to justice."

In a series of speeches, Harris positions herself as the Leader of a Free World engaged in an existential battle with the forces of absolute Evil. In close coordination with President Macron and other leaders of the Coalition of the Willing, she makes all key decisions regarding the delivery of state-of-the-art Western aircraft and technical specialists to Ukraine. At the end of October, she pays a triumphant visit to Kyiv, the capital city of embattled Ukraine.

By November 5th, a candidate named Trump with his treasonous plan will have faded into the background as a brilliant black woman, dubbed the Churchill of the 21st century by the world media, steps to the fore.

This is more or less what I see as the Free World's last chance to overcome the widespread dementia of its leaders.

Still Time to Save US and Ukraine from Putin and His "Western" Stooges

First published on July 16th, 2024

Donald Trump has just picked as his running mate Senator J. D. Vance, a fierce and pathological hater of Ukraine and a key organizer of a recent five-month blockade of military deliveries to Ukraine. Vance is unlikely to bring many new votes into Trump's camp but rather alienate some moderates.

His nomination is a personal challenge to an influential group of Reagan School republicans (McCaul, Rogers, Turner) who laid out their vision for the war in a remarkable document—the "Proposed Plan for Victory in Ukraine."

So the choice of his running mate, senseless from electoral prospects, revealed once again Trump's "mysterious" psychological addiction to the despot in the Kremlin. Trump's latest political gaffe makes my idea (elaborated in the previous column) on how to stop Trump and consequently win a World War even more urgent, more appropriate, and more promising (!). Briefly, the recipe for overcoming the looming disaster for all of us:

- For reasons of health, Biden should not only step aside as a candidate but resign the presidency as well.
- Becoming President of the United States would considerably expand the electoral potential of a new candidate Kamala Harris.
- On day one, President Harris includes the Republican Proposed Plan for Victory in Ukraine in her campaign platform as its key strategic element.
- In a series of speeches, Harris positions herself as the Leader of a Free World engaged in an existential battle with the forces of

absolute Evil. She passionately denounces Putin-Orban-Trump-Vance's disgusting "peace plan" as a conspiracy to destroy Ukraine.

- In close coordination with President Macron and other leaders of the Coalition of the Willing, she makes all key decisions regarding the delivery of state-of-the-art Western aircraft and technical specialists to Ukraine.

- At the end of October, she pays a triumphant visit to Kyiv, the capital city of gallant Ukraine.

Choosing Best US Strategy Towards Russia and Ukraine

First published on August 5th, 2024

At one of the most critical moments for the current Biden administration (after his disastrous June debate), I proposed a strategy that would allow him to win both the US elections and the World War unleashed by Vladimir Putin's Empire of Evil against the Free World.

The strategy I proposed boiled down to three decisive steps:

- For health reasons, Biden should step aside as both a candidate and resign the presidency; allowing Kamala Harris to assume the presidency before the election would considerably expand what she would offer as a candidate.
- On day one, President Harris complies with the requirement to provide Congress with her administration's objectives for the war in Ukraine by proclaiming the McCaul-Rogers-Turner Proposed Plan for Victory in Ukraine as an official, bi-partisan US victory plan.
- In implementing this plan President Harris would position herself as the Leader of the Free World, engaged in an existential battle with the forces of absolute evil. In close coordination with President Macron and other leaders of the Coalition of the Willing, she would make all key decisions regarding the prompt delivery of state-of-the-art Western aircraft and technical specialists to Ukraine. (150-200 planes).

As of today, the first step of this proposed strategy has been partially implemented, a step that has turned this election campaign around for the Democrats. It will now be a close contest as both sides make their pitches to undecided voters.

Many Pro-Ukraine Republicans are now among these undecided voters; mere hours after Biden stepped aside as a presidential candidate, The Nikki Haley Votes PAC called its followers to support Kamala Harris.

Haley voters are currently unhappy. First, they heard about alleged "consultations" on a peace deal for Ukraine involving Trump and Putin, with Orbán as a mediator. Then Trump chose J. D. Vance, a rabid "Ukrainophobe," as his running mate.

To keep Ukraine supporters in their orbit, Republican strategists have initiated a discussion on various versions of the "Trump plan" that looks more or less favorably on Ukraine. The version that has gained the most traction is the "Pompeo plan."

Mike Pompeo served as Secretary of State in the Trump Cabinet—a crucial role to say the least. His predecessor, Rex Tillerson, never hit it off with Trump, after referring to him as a moron in public, he eventually resigned, slamming the door behind him as he left.

Pompeo saw his role as much more far-reaching and constructive. He was a kind of wise mentor encouraging the novice's positive foreign policy instincts towards the Middle East, and played the role of attentive nursemaid, cleaning up after Trump's diplomatic missteps, such as his relationship with NATO. Pompeo was also more diplomatic than Tillerson—instead of referring to his boss as a moron, he came up with the term "alternative genius."

Mike Pompeo is an ardent Atlanticist. He supports Ukraine and, if Trump wins another term in office, hopes to play the same role of wise guardian within the administration. His plan can be summed up as follows: 1) both sides agree to a cease-fire along the existing entire line of contact. They agree to nothing else. NATO, either collectively or led by the leading member states, take on responsibility for defending every inch of Ukrainian territory on the Western side of the cease-fire line. 2) Putin would be welcome, of course, to test these obligations in any way he sees fit, but he knows full well what the consequences will be. The West will meanwhile never recognize the territory currently held by Moscow's forces and proxies as legally belonging to Russia.

It's a solid plan. In essence, we are talking about accepting a divided country into NATO (as West Germany in 1955). But the plan has two major flaws.

Firstly, it's Pompeo's plan and not Trump's. The latter's mysterious psychological addiction to the dictator in the Kremlin has not waned in the slightest and is bound to produce a wealth of surprises.

Secondly, why should Ukraine have to pay such a hefty price to guarantee its security? We are talking about the occupation of 20 percent of its territory to continue for several more years. As I see it, no one seems to truly grasp the logical structure of this war; not Pompeo; not these vaunted military experts.

They proceed from a belief that the conflict has reached a stalemate—a war of attrition—and that neither side is capable of breaking through the front line. The Russians not only will never make it to Kyiv; they won't even take Kharkiv. In the same vein Ukrainians will never fight their way back to the borders of 1991 and liberate all occupied territory. This is all true.

Ukraine has another path to victory.

The Russian-Ukrainian war is not merely a deadlocked confrontation along the thousand-kilometer line of contact. The war has a completely different center of gravity (cf. Clausewitz)—the Crimean Peninsula. Both sides highly value the political symbolism of Crimea which, at the same time, represents the most vulnerable component of Russia's military machine. Ukraine managed to dislodge Moscow's naval forces from its Crimean ports while lacking aircraft or a naval fleet. And now, having received long-range missiles, Ukraine has been striking airfields in the Crimea on a regular basis—it turns out that Russian air defense systems are inadequate.

If the skies over Ukraine become dotted with 100, or, even better, 200 state-of-the-art Western aircraft, the country will not only gain supremacy in the air but will also render Russia's occupation of the Crimea untenable. Moscow will have to withdraw from the peninsula or be completely destroyed from afar.

The loss of Crimea would result in the political (and potentially physical) death of Vladimir Putin and an end to the war.

The "Proposed Plan for Victory in Ukraine" is much preferable to Pompeo's. This Republican (McCaul, Roger, Turner) Plan represents the best strategy for Harris to win the election and consequently win the World War that some fear is inevitable.

Letter to the Editor— A Further Tribute to Peter Reddaway

First published on August 11th, 2024

Dear Bohdan Nahaylo!

Thank you so much for your very thorough and moving "In Memoriam" devoted to our outstanding contemporary Peter Reddaway who passed away several weeks ago. He was both a scholar and a visionary.

I would like to share some previously unrevealed details regarding the considerable political and spiritual impact he had on events which transpired in the post-Soviet space during the critical years of 1989-1991.

All Soviet dissidents, as well as many of our friends in the West, were of course familiar with Andrei Amalric's brilliant essay "Will the Soviet Union Survive until 1984?" (1970). All of us knew his famous verdict by heart: "Just as the adoption of Christianity prolonged the existence of the Roman Empire for 300 years, so the adoption of communism extended the existence of the Russian empire for several decades."

In 1989, as Amalric's prophetic words became a reality before our very eyes, I came across a Peter Reddaway article analyzing this dramatic process. I was particularly impressed by one of his Amalric-esque observations on the nature of the Soviet empire.

"The Soviet incarnation of the Russian Empire," argued Reddaway, "is radically different from the British or French empires. Its metropole is not Russia like France and Britain in the case of their empires. It is (according to Amalric) an ideocratic quasi-religious empire and its metropole does not have a territorial nature. Its metropole are ideological institutions and security agencies imposed on every nation of the USSR, including Russia."

At that time, (1989-1991) I happened to be a kind of informal adviser to Boris Yeltsin. I organized his visit to Tbilisi after the April 9, 1989, massacre (the first attempt by the imperial metropole to crush the national aspirations of a Soviet republic by force).

On returning to Moscow, Yeltsin delivered one of his best speeches at the "Congress of People's Deputies of the USSR," where he blamed Gorbachev and his imperial entourage directly: "I was there, I saw it with my own eyes. It was a crime. A crime committed by the Soviet state against its own people."

I shared Amalric and Reddaway's ideas with Boris Nikolaevich and he wholeheartedly agreed with them. But that's not all—he was inspired to mold a very organic and creative (and, as it turned out, hugely successful) model of political self-presentation.

From the spring of 1989, Yeltsin began positioning himself as a national leader, a rebel striving for the independence of his country—Russia—from the USSR, an old and decrepit ideocratic communist empire. From this political perspective, all the leaders of the national liberation movements in Ukraine, Georgia, and the Baltic Republics were in essence becoming his brothers-in-arms.

In 1990 and 1991, imperial proponents attempted to stop the dissolution of the Soviet empire by force. Each time that happened, Boris Yeltsin, as President of the Russian Federation (elected in June 1990), used his considerable political clout to thwart them.

One of the more dramatic events along these lines transpired in January 1991, when the KGB seized the Lithuanian TV Center (thirteen people died). The President of the Russian Federation immediately rushed to Vilnius, then to Tallinn, finally to Riga. There he co-signed, along with the leaders of all three Baltic Republics, treaties on the mutual recognition of each republic's independence. His actions were then supported in Moscow by the largest ever (approximately one million participants) anti-communist, anti-imperial demonstration for Lithuanian independence.

The Peter Reddaway idea of mother-Russia rebelling against the Soviet empire alongside other republics was able to unify Russian society. The concept appealed both to the Eurocentric aspirations of liberals as well as to the patriotic feelings of those with a nationalist bent.

Yeltsin was extremely popular in those years. He was generally perceived as a genuinely Russian leader. On June 13, 1990, the Russian Parliament adopted "The Declaration of Independence for the Russian Federation" nearly unanimously. Liberal and Nationalist deputies embraced each other after the vote. This was essentially a Declaration Dissolving the Empire. It certainly dissolved the Eurasian Empire which had existed for more than seven centuries, in various incarnations (Ulus Jochi, the Russian Empire, the Soviet Union).

Students sometimes ask me who the author of this Declaration of Russian Independence was. I always reply: Professor Peter Reddaway. Thanks to his ideas, the process of the dissolution of the Soviet Empire (1989-1991) proceeded relatively smoothly. Think for a moment about a similar case: the break-up of that mini-empire in the south—Yugoslavia.

It took three decades for the imperial metropole to take revenge on Russia and unleash a crazy, doomed war, setting the stage for the 4th incarnation of a fallen Empire—Русский Мир.

Ukraine's Counter-Invasion of Russia's Kursk Region May Decide the War

First published on August 15th, 2024

The Kursk Operation carried out by the Ukrainian Armed Forces may play the deciding role in the outcome of the Russo-Ukrainian war.

The Ukrainians just need to keep applying the pressure and do it in the proper manner. From a tactical standpoint, they have achieved a major military victory—that cannot be disputed. But the more far-reaching success has been a strategic and psychological one, and it has impacted decision-makers in both Washington and Moscow.

"Bold, brilliant, beautiful," is how US Senator Lindsey Graham (R-SC) described Ukraine's cross-border operation during a bi-partisan Senate delegation visit to Kyiv on Monday. US Senator Richard Blumenthal (D-CT) called it "historic" and a "seismic breakthrough."

But the senators went further than mere congratulatory remarks. Imagine my delight when I discovered that the two gentlemen had, in their final communique, articulated "My Theory for Delivering Victory to Ukraine," which I have presented to readers in a series of articles in the Kyiv Post.

Senators Blumenthal and Graham issued a joint, bipartisan communique after their visit: "After listening to President Zelensky, we urge the Biden Administration to lift restrictions on weapons provided by the United States so they can strike the Russian invaders more effectively. . . . Additionally, President Zelensky told us both that he would be looking to supplement his Air Force by establishing a program to recruit retired NATO F-16 fighter pilots. We support this effort. Ukraine is already fielding units of freedom fighters on the ground, and this volunteer force should be replicated in the air."

The overly cautious, fainthearted West has clearly grown bolder, and that's without Macron weighing in yet. He is only now emerging from the informal truce agreed to for the Olympic games in Paris.

The biggest threat now for Putin and his associates inside Russia comes not from anti-war liberals (their leaders have either been killed, exiled, or thrown in jail) but from the Z-patriot scum demanding that this bloody ballet continue. This crowd has become more and more suspicious of late— whispers of "The Tsar is not Real!" grow louder. The debacle in Kursk may see these suspicions turn to certainties.

Our sorry excuse for a fuhrer knows perfectly well that the World War he unleashed on the West on February 24, 2022—"Take your stuff and get out of here, out of the pages of world history"—has been lost. He lost it at the Battle of Hostomel and will never assume the mantle of Master of the Universe.

Putin's main problem at present is an existential one—how to remain in power (and, thus, alive) in a country that has lost a war. As a possible solution to this problem, he began arresting generals by the dozen and blaming them for the defeat.

What of poor Gerasimov, sitting in some basement swearing to the dictator he would drive out the Ukrainian occupiers by the end of his workday? I fear we have seen the last of him.

The Kursk debacle has forced me to make a few corrections to my plan for victory for Ukraine. My initial version, supported by the US Congressional Delegation on August 12th in Kyiv, stipulated that Ukraine would receive 150-200 state-of-the-art Western aircraft and that the enemy's alignment of forces in Crimea be destroyed remotely. On a practical level, two to three months would be needed to implement this plan. It seems recent events have significantly lowered the regime's life expectancy.

We already have ten F-16 fighter aircraft which could be equipped with Storm Shadow and SCALP missiles. We have ATACMS with a range of 300 km (186 miles). I believe these assets would be sufficient to blow the Crimea bridge to smithereens, and it would take a mere two to three weeks to plan. We might even be able to do it before the end of August, the traditional month for the collapse of Russian regimes.

In the public consciousness, destroying a crucial symbol of Rashist expansionism, coupled with the disgrace in Kursk, will do much to detonate that flammable mixture of a second-rate fuhrer, a second-rate military, and second-rate patriots. The Z-patriot scum and ex-cons will then bolt out of the trenches of Kursk and Donbas, armed to the teeth, and head straight to the address printed on the murdered Prigozhin's final pamphlets—to the Rublyovka estates of the well-fed oligarchs and generals who unleashed this senseless war.

The meltdown of Russian society has already begun and is no longer possible to stop. At the cost of thousands upon thousands of lives, Ukraine has managed to prevent the Rashist magma from spreading to prosperous Europe. The individuals and institutions laying claim to the role of "Leader of the Free World" can and must help Ukraine immediately in purging its sovereign territory of the toxic by-products of the collapse of Russian statehood.

Ukraine's Audacity

First published on August 28th, 2024

"Audacity, audacity, and more audacity, and the Fatherland will be saved," French Revolutionary Georges Danton said in 1792. And audacity is what Ukraine demonstrates as it carries out a revolution in world geopolitics before the eyes of a stunned and mesmerized world. Ukraine is defying not only its deadly Russian enemy but also its cowardly Western allies.

Not only physical, but primarily intellectual and spiritual courage enabled Ukraine to become de facto a leader of the Free World. A bipartisan US Senate delegation headed by American foreign policy veterans such as Lindsey Graham (R) and Richard Blumenthal (D), which arrived in Kyiv on August 12th, was youthfully relaxed, glowing with genuine enthusiasm, and the senators did not skimp on the most enthusiastic appraisals of the Ukrainian Army's Kursk operation: "Bold, brilliant, beautiful, a historic seismic breakthrough."

For over a half year, your humble servant, a so-called "urban madman," has been proposing to the Free World a simple and convincing plan for victory in the Fourth World War against the Empire of Absolute Evil. The West will provide Ukraine with 150-200 modern airplanes, whose crews are composed of the best NATO aces, including a few dozen Ukrainian pilots who have undergone special training. The aggressor's land grouping, following its Black Sea Fleet, will leave the Crimean Peninsula under threat of long-distance destruction. Or it is destroyed.

In Kyiv on August 12th, in an uplifting post-Kursk atmosphere, practically the same plan was proposed by three much more influential "urban madmen"—Volodymyr Zelensky, Lindsey Graham, and Richard Blumenthal (with the replacement of NATO aces by "retired NATO F-16 fighter pilots").

Old man Biden would never go for this plan. (Incidentally, I am convinced that the Ukrainian military-political leadership prepared the Kursk operation in total secrecy, purposely keeping the details from its main ally. Otherwise, it definitely would have been thwarted.)

Kamala Harris, however, very much wants to become the US president. Biden's departure changed the presidential race from a hopeless one for the Democrats to a situation of uncertainty with roughly equal chances for both sides.

The majority of both Democratic and Republican voters have already made up their minds. The elections will be determined by the independents, the undecided, the doubters. Both candidates have to fight for these votes. In the current elections, a new cluster of such voters has appeared—pro-Ukrainian Republicans. Those who voted in the primaries for Nikki Haley; those who proposed their own Ukrainian Victory plan to Congress (Michael McCall, Mike Rogers, Mike Turner); those who together with Graham and Blumenthal are now demanding that the administration immediately supply Ukraine with airplanes and NATO crews. If the collective Harris makes this historic decision while the moron Donald Trump continues to discuss NATO expansion with the equally moronic Elon Musk, then the Republican Reaganites will vote for Harris.

But Ukraine will not wait with bated breath to see what policy the adult aunties and uncles in Washington will adopt. As the sole country fighting today for the entire flourishing Free World, Ukraine has the right, and, most importantly also, the opportunity to shape American policy, and that of other nations. At the Kyiv meeting, the senators justifiably called the effect of the Kursk operation on Western public awareness seismic, but they did not imagine the degree of its influence on the consciousness of Russian society.

First, a few words about the attitude of today's Russian society to the war. No one today has precise sociological data. I adhere to a rough working scheme: up to 15 percent of the population, inculcated with fascist propaganda, are Z-rabble, die-hard Russian imperialists. Approximately the same percentage in Russia are principled opponents of the criminal war. The remaining 70 percent, according to the classic formulation of our great poet Pushkin, are silent (bezmolvstvuyt). Today, when all leading opponents of the war have been killed, exiled, or imprisoned, only the Z-scum party dominates the informational and political expanse. The regime's total crackdown on the liberal opposition, however, led to a paradoxical result: politics returned to Russia. A growing crisis is evident within the party in power itself.

A vague suspicion that long ago was already smoldering within this fascist party—"The Tsar is a fake!"—is spreading after the Kursk operation like wildfire through administration Telegram channels and the TV studios of the Kremlin propagandists after the Kursk operation. In the course of this entertaining process, the lower ranks of the war party are discovering that not only the tsar but also their kingdom is not real, and they are starting to recall Prigozhin's pamphlets just before his death denouncing "oligarchs and generals living it up in Rublyovka."

As for the generals, the tsar himself is not sparing them either, arresting them today by the dozen for theft in order tomorrow to blame them for defeat and to charge them with treason.

A fake tsar, whose red lines were crossed first by audacious Ukraine and then very cautiously also by the West; dim-witted, alcoholic Russian generals, dispatched as in the purges in 1937 one after the other to the Chekist cellars; the Z-rabble deceived in their fascist imperial fantasies—this is the combustible mixture of the Russian political scene, ready to explode at any moment.

Now, when the Ukrainian Victory Plan is in the reliable hands of the bipartisan pro-Ukrainian majority of the US Congress the majority of Western observers consider that a new air armada will appear in Ukrainian skies in approximately two-three months.

For the second time in a short space of time, however, Ukraine may pleasantly surprise the entire world. I assume that Ukraine already has a sufficient number of modern planes (at least 10-20) and long-range missiles to completely destroy the hated symbol of the fascist occupation—the Crimean Bridge. In two to three weeks. Or two to three days, for example.

Observing the Russian "political scene," every day I become more and more convinced about the self-destructive chain reaction this explosion will evoke inside the Russian political establishment. Perhaps it won't even be necessary to call up the NATO pensioners from their deserved rest.

The Candidates' Debate Will Take Place under Grandpa Biden's Shadow

First published on September 9th, 2024

Kamala Harris has achieved a great deal in the month or so since she entered the race for the presidency. She has erased Trump's five-point lead in the polls for both national and key battleground states. The American electorate now seems much more comfortable with the thought of Harris as potential president, a feat she has been able to accomplish without projecting any overly exceptional qualities or coming up with any groundbreaking proposals.

It simply became clear a posteriori that a matchup between Trump and Biden was essentially a competition of their unfavorability ratings. So when one of these candidates was "shown the door," so to speak, the less-than-ideal Kamala Harris suddenly had the advantage.

This turn of events couldn't help but knock Trump off his game when his chances of victory increased considerably every time the hapless Biden appeared in public. Now, in order to regain the lead, he will have to deliver a knockout blow at the September 10th debate, much as he did two months ago with Biden.

Trump's usual obnoxiousness will not be enough to deliver a knockout this time around. He needs to take a more substantive approach. Judging from his recent statements on the Middle East, his advisers perceive this topic to be a weak spot for Democrats and have armed their candidate with strong talking points in the run up to the debate.

Trump has essentially accused the Biden administration of betraying its most important ally in the Middle East. One can argue with the wording of the sentiment, but it is nonetheless increasingly difficult to parse the outgoing president's endless sputtering about "avoiding a war at all costs," or how crucial it is to "keep this conflict from escalating into a regional war."

Honestly, what escalation? What regional war is the presumed "Leader of the Free World" afraid of when the forces of Absolute Evil (Russia, Iran, North Korea) are already waging a genocidal world war against the Free World with the aim of exterminating two of its freedom-loving nations: Ukraine and Israel.

I have two recommendations for Madam Vice-President. The first is she must somewhat distance herself from the current president. In the two months that remain in the campaign, she cannot allow herself to be held responsible for every new statement or decision emanating from the White House. She needs to remind both her opponent and American voters that her last name is Harris, not Biden, and to do all she can to articulate a more pro-Israel position.

She can further distance herself from Grandpa Biden by refusing to accommodate the Hamas apologists within the Democratic Party—both the progressives and the Islamists. She will lose their votes, yes, but in return gain ground with mainstream voters, three quarters of whom are in favor of more support for Israel.

After aligning herself more or less with Trump's pro-Israel stance, Harris would have sufficient cover to launch a decisive counterattack. She would be fully justified in calling out Trump's hypocrisy as well as his pathetic, shameful groveling before the serial killer in the Kremlin.

Case in point: Trump rightly criticizes Biden for not showing sufficient support for Israel, but then in the same breath claims that Biden's unchecked support for Ukraine has brought the world to the brink of nuclear war.

Trump is nothing if not consistent in his aggressive hatred of Ukraine. Politicians in his corner in Congress made sure to block a military aid package to Ukraine for more than six months, putting the country in grave danger of losing the war. Trump then chose the most enthusiastic of these lowlifes to be his running mate.

The Republican establishment's position on Ukraine, however, differs drastically from that of Trump. The chairmen of the three most prominent House Committees have already submitted a "Proposed Plan for Victory in Ukraine" for Congressional review.

The Ukrainian military's incursion into Kursk was met with widespread approval and enthusiasm in Congress. During a bipartisan Congressional delegation visit to Kyiv led by Senators Graham and Blumenthal, the two lawmakers characterized the operation as "bold, brilliant, beautiful." In addition, after their meeting with President Volodymyr Zelensky, the senators stated they would urge the US administration to agree to the Ukrainian president's persistent suggestions to:

- Remove all restrictions on strikes on the interior of Russian territory using American weapons.
- Provide Ukraine with additional air defense assets.
- Provide Ukraine with a significant, "game-changing" number of state-of-the-art aircraft flown by volunteer NATO pilots.

Zelensky has announced he is going to Washington, DC on September 22nd and will take with him his Plan for Victory. He intends to discuss its implementation with Biden, Harris, and Trump.

The September 10th candidates' debate will offer Harris a perfect opportunity to show not only the President of Ukraine but also the whole world just who of the three is most up to the task; who, quoting the Russian poet Fedor Tyutchev, is willing "in moments of destiny" to assume the mantle of Leader of the Free World.

Ukraine is looking forward to hearing the following words from Kamala Harris on September 22: "Thank you, Mr. President. I accept your Plan. It is now Our Plan for Our Victory."

Unfortunately, Kyiv is unlikely to hear such enthusiasm from Trump or Biden.

And last but not least, all this will do much to sway the largest current group of undecideds—pro-Ukraine Republicans—to vote for Harris and ensure she wins on Nov. 5.

After the Debate

First published on September 15th, 2024

In my pre-debate column I took the liberty of offering the US vice-president two recommendations:

- distance herself from the current president, Joseph Biden
- denounce as strongly as possible Trump's treasonous relationship with Putin as it concerns the war in Ukraine

It seems Harris's advisers agreed with me as they prepped her for the debate. More surprisingly, perhaps . . . so did her opponent. The rejoinder "my last name is Harris, not Biden" became a running theme during the night, not the least because Trump kept leaving himself open for it. But the former president truly outdid himself when it came to my second recommendation. Harris didn't even need to bring up anything he has said in the past. Trump himself spewed all the crap Putin has fed him over the years (including the stuff about Orban) in real time and at length. He even went so far as to echo Putin's nuclear blackmail of the United States when he accused Biden of bringing the country to the brink of nuclear war "with his unchecked support for Ukraine."

The vast majority of voters from both parties have already made up their minds. The outcome of the election will be determined by the undecideds, and the two candidates will be forced to fight for their votes. A new group of undecided voters has taken shape in this election cycle—pro-Ukraine Republicans. They voted for Haley in the primaries, they came up with the "Plan for Victory in Ukraine" and submitted it to Congress (McCaul, Rogers, Turner), and they agree with Senators Graham and Blumenthal that the current administration must immediately allow Ukraine to strike Russia's interior using American weapons and provide Kyiv with aircraft flown by NATO pilots.

Mike McCaul, Chairman of the House Foreign Affairs Committee and the informal leader of the bipartisan pro-Ukraine majority in Congress, recently made public an open letter he addressed to the White House: "As long as it is conducting its brutal, full-scale war of aggression, Russia must not be given a sanctuary from which it can execute its war crimes against Ukraine with impunity."

What's more, McCaul stated the night before the debate that he had spoken with Secretary of State Blinken and that Blinken had promised him he would announce the lifting of strike restrictions on Ukraine during his September 11th visit to Kyiv. Something prevented Blinken from fulfilling his promise to lawmakers, however, as he again asked for more time so he could return to Washington and brief Biden.

The next few days in Washington will prove decisive not only for the upcoming election but for the outcome of the war currently waging across the globe. If Grandpa Biden decides to flap his gums again about how it's "unacceptable for this conflict to escalate," then how is he any better than Trump the nuclear blackmailer and what use was it for Harris to denounce her opponent's treasonous stance on Ukraine during the debate!?

They might as well just kiss Trump's ass and give the Manchurian Candidate the keys to the White House while they're at it.

Kamala Harris showed the world that she is capable of winning on November 5th. The key to victory? Pro-Ukraine Republicans. Mike McCaul has articulated their position perfectly. It could not be further from Trump's pro-Putin stance. If Grandpa Biden prevents Harris from adopting McCaul's "Plan for Victory In Ukraine," the Democratic Party's unofficial politburo might need to step in again and urge him to make yet another tough decision—this time to resign from office.

Hic Rhodus, hic salta

First published on September 22nd, 2024

According to most post-debate polls, Democrat candidate Kamala Harris has increased her slight lead over Republican candidate Donald Trump by a few percentage points both on the national level and in key swing states. The remaining months of the campaign will see the two US presidential candidates fight to sway the undecided voters.

What's different this election cycle is the appearance of a new group of these undecideds—pro-Ukraine Republicans who voted for Nikki Haley in the primaries and who support Republican Congressman Mike McCaul's demands on the administration to immediately remove all restrictions on strikes deep within the territory of the aggressor state using American weapons.

Harris realizes the key to her victory is to bring this group of voters to her side. She has spent a huge amount of advertisement money in swing states, touting her support for Ukraine and attacking the Trumps (both father and son) over their blatantly traitorous remarks on the war, as well as Republican vice president nominee J. D. Vance and that disgraced offspring of the Kennedy clan, RFK Jr.

But this powerful, focused campaign strategy is being undermined as we speak by sheer stubbornness on the part of Grandpa Biden, who keeps dragging his ancient feet in lifting the ban on strikes within Russia's interior using American weapons.

This may all change, thankfully, next week in Washington—Ukrainian President Volodymyr Zelensky is due to arrive with his Plan for Victory. These high-level meetings may prove decisive, not only for the outcome of the US election but—and this is much more important—for the global conflict waging throughout the world as well.

Experts are divided on the purely military aspects of Ukraine's incursion into Russia's Kursk region, but no one can deny it has had an enormous political and psychological impact. Both Washington and Moscow have now completely altered their perceptions of the war. A significant portion of the US political establishment now believes Ukraine can really win this war.

In August, a bipartisan congressional delegation met with Zelensky in Kyiv and negotiated the general parameters of this Plan for Victory (the elimination of red lines on using American weapons and the delivery of a substantial number of state-of-the-art fighter planes flown by volunteer Western pilots). In the run-up to Zelensky's visit, McCaul and his colleagues have been lobbying hard for the plan in Washington.

In Moscow, the powers that be continue their relentless hunt for those opposing the war, punishing them for social media posts or even a stray "like." However, after Ukraine's Kursk incursion, Russian President Vladimir Putin has gained a potentially much more dangerous adversary, namely his previous base of support—the Z-patriot community. This group is now condemning the president, not for starting an illegal war but for, in their view, beginning to lose it.

The Z-military correspondents post constantly on their Telegram channels and video blogs. But now, alongside their usual criticisms of "Ukrofascists" and the accursed West, we are seeing angry exposes about rampant theft in the military, the incompetence of military leaders, and the harsh treatment of subordinates. Muted suspicions that "The tsar is not real!" are beginning to grow louder.

The entire saga with Prigozhin, who remains popular with the Z-patriot community, reminds us how quickly sentiments such as "[Sergei] Shoigu is a stupid ass! [Valery] Gerasimov is such a jackass! Where is our ammunition?" can result in a military uprising and a march on Moscow.

In a desperate attempt to prevent the White House from removing those red lines to make things easier for Ukraine, Putin is again resorting to that favorite weapon of terrorists the world over—blackmail. We are now hearing almost daily from the Kremlin that if Ukraine is permitted to conduct strikes deep within its territory, Russia will consider itself at war with all of NATO.

But Zelensky made himself perfectly clear at a joint press conference in Kyiv with European Commission President Ursula von der Leyen on September 20th. He first addressed directly those close to Biden who are urging him to give in to Putin's blackmail. Zelensky had in mind, of course, CIA Director William J. Burns, who made a secret verbal agreement with Putin in Moscow in November 2021. In essence, Burns is continuing to fulfill this treasonous 2021 agreement with Putin to this day.

Zelensky also made sure to mention that in addition to his meetings in Washington with Biden, Harris and Trump, he will meet with the Congress as well. And on the eve of his departure, Zelensky gained yet another powerful ally in his quest to pressure Biden—Europe. The vast majority of the newly elected European Parliament has called for all restrictions on strikes deep within Russian territory using Western weapons to be lifted.

We have every reason to believe that these restrictions will be lifted by the end of the week. As a result, Putin will become victim number one of his own blackmail. So, he announces he is at war with NATO? Great, Vladimir Vladimirovich! Hic Rhodus, hic salta!

But I have a feeling that won't happen against an alliance with vastly superior conventional weapons. Especially considering French President Emmanuel Macron has already politely pointed out that France, too, has nuclear weapons.

The Z-patriot community will surely be most disappointed in its one-time "vozhd."[6]

---

6   A Slavic word meaning "the leader" —Ed.

Invite Ukraine to Join NATO Now

First published on October 29th, 2024

It's been almost three years now since Ukraine began its heroic and single-handed defense of the prosperous and hedonistic West from an invasion at the hands of 21st century barbarians. The entire "civilized world" has looked on as Ukraine bleeds out on the battlefield while these barbarians attempt to humiliate and destroy this very same West. Meanwhile, US administration officials and other Western politicians have held discussion after discussion over these three years to try to clarify just what their goal is in the Russo-Ukrainian war—a Victory for Ukraine or simply a No Defeat?

The most common talking point we hear in these discussions amounts to a perpetual mantra more than anything else: "The most important thing to remember is that we must prevent this conflict from escalating. We must do all we can to keep it from turning into a regional war."

While this pathetic blathering continues to fill the air, the West's mortal enemies—the tyrannical regimes in Russia, Iran, North Korea, and China have managed to unleash World War IV against it. (With a personal stamp of approval from the UN General Secretary, incidentally)

It's hard not to notice how invigorated the war criminal in Moscow has become of late after obtaining an almost unlimited (as many as the sands on the sounding shore[7]) supply of brainwashed potential soldiers to mobilize. They are straight out of Blok's poem—the "slit-eyed greedy-looking Asians ready to burn our cities down and roast their white-skinned brethren alive."

Putin's latest escalation with North Korea serves as an inflection point within the current world war and reminds one of Stalin's escalation with China in October 1950 during the Cold War (World War III). How the West and the Free World (if this term means anything at all anymore) choose to

---

7   From Aleksandr Blok's poem "The Scythians" (1918).

react to this escalation will determine both the outcome of the war and the course of history for the rest of the 21st century.

But first a few comments regarding the very nature of the Russo-Ukrainian war. The structure of the conflict is really a dynamic superposition of two very different wars. The first of these is a classic war of attrition along the thousand-kilometer line of contact between the two sides. Here theoretically Russia has the advantage due to two factors: its larger mobilization potential and the low value that Russian society places on human life. And now we have the Korean factor coming into play as well.

But the Russian military machine has one vulnerable area—the Crimean peninsula. The struggle to control it constitutes, as Carl von Clausewitz put it, the psychological center of gravity of the entire Russo-Ukrainian war. With this second component, Ukraine has already demonstrated a clear superiority. Without a navy or state-of-the-art aircraft, Ukraine managed to oust the Black Sea Fleet from Sevastopol and on a daily basis strikes Russian military targets throughout the peninsula.

Ukraine's path to victory is a transparent and logical one:

The West must get rid of its most absurd red line, one they placed on themselves: the requirement that any modern Western aircraft supplied to Ukraine be operated exclusively by pilots with Ukrainian passports. First of all, this almost suicidal restriction has prolonged an already devastating war for two years. Secondly, if we continue to blindly adhere to it, the best we can hope for is 30-40 random airplanes, hardly a game-changer in this conflict.

In order to truly turn the tide in this conflict, Ukraine needs 150 aircraft. Not just individual airplanes but cohesive squadrons of, if not American F-16s, then Mirages from France, Typhoons from the UK, or Gripens from Sweden. Then we would see Russia's entire alignment of forces placed under threat of a long-range impending attack. It would result in more than the navy fleeing the peninsula.

The Ukrainian flag flying over Sevastopol would result in a catastrophic defeat for Russia, and, at the very least, the political death of the blood-sucker in the Kremlin.

This Victory Plan has support from France, the UK, and a bipartisan majority within the US Congress, both the outgoing one and the one to be elected on November 5th. Only, Mr. Biden, "We must prevent war at all costs!" is withholding his support.

With each passing day, Kamala Harris loses another opportunity to distance herself from the president on the issue of Ukraine (if nothing else, she should call for the ban on strikes on Russia's interior to be lifted) and in so doing gain the support of a significant block of undecided Republican voters who are pro-Ukraine. The proposals put forth by Trump and Vance do not bode well for Ukraine either.

The skies over Iran on the night of October 26th showed the world that the Horde's air defense systems are far inferior to the West's state-of-the-art aviation. The fact remains that the West could simply snap its fingers and guarantee a victory for Ukraine, a victory it itself sorely needs. Instead, it forces Ukraine to shed even more rivers of blood in pursuit of a victory for all. While they trod this heroic path, however, Ukrainians might simply cease to exist at all.

When the political situation becomes clearer in the US on November 6th, the collective West and the US administration need to come to a strategic decision.

Either Ukraine receives an air armada capable of liberating the Crimea or Ukraine is forced to agree to two things: a cease-fire along the line of contact proposed by China and Brazil, and a willingness to negotiate with Russia. Because without an air force, Ukraine's position in a classic war of attrition will only worsen.

The key word in all this is "negotiations." What Putin wants to negotiate is abundantly clear—the destruction of Ukrainian statehood and morphing a territorial entity with its capital in Kyiv (which he was unable to take in 7 or 1007 days) into a Russian protectorate. The achieving of this goal, as envisioned by the war criminal in the Kremlin, would be a key point of the agreement. It would guarantee that Ukraine would remain utterly vulnerable in the face of a new round of aggression from Muscovy—"Ukraine will refrain from ever joining NATO."

It seems Putin is willing to make major concessions on almost all other issues, including territorial ones. Because does it really matter if this or that Ukrainian oblast belongs explicitly to Muscovy or to the protectorate subordinate to it?

This is why Ukraine and the West, if they agree to the China/Brazil initiative, must unequivocally reject Putin's wishlist both de jure and de facto before engaging in any negotiations.

The best way to do this would be to offer Ukraine an immediate invitation to join NATO. This is a crucial procedural step which every applicant nation must take; after it is completed the admissions process is virtually irreversible.

As for how prepared Ukraine is to join the alliance, let us remember that Ukraine is the only nation in the world, in the seventy-five year history of the organization, that has been fulfilling the very function for which NATO was founded—the destruction of the Eurasian horde crashing towards civilized Europe.

But, wait, you say, if that happens Putin won't agree to the China/Brazil initiative. No temporary gains in territory will mitigate one fundamental loss for him: Ukraine (even if it's not the entire country's territory for the time being) will have gone over for good to the West—to NATO and the EU. The tsar will automatically become a false one for the Z-blogosphere scum.

Okay, so say he doesn't agree to the initiative. Then what can he do? Bring on ten or twenty thousand deranged Koreans and lead them to burn our cities down and roast their white-skinned brethren alive?

I think in this case, the "white-skinned brethren" in the White House will not wait around for a verbatim culmination of Blok's prophecy and resolve, finally, to dispatch flight crews to Ukraine composed of volunteer pilots.

P. S. Several of these issues were discussed at the recent G4 summit in Berlin. A source maintains that these discussions made clear that twenty-five out of thirty-two NATO members are in favor of offering Ukraine an invitation to join the alliance right now. They are also in favor of letting Ukraine use Western pilots. The deciding negative note came from the US. As the discussions continued, the US softened its stance somewhat. Its representative made it known that if Harris wins in November, he would side with the majority on both issues. Why only if Harris wins, Mister President? If Trump wins, you will still be fully in charge for another two months or so. And you will then face a huge, epic responsibility. You will have to make an irreversible decision, one that obligates the next president and secures a victory for the Free World over the Empire of Absolute Evil. In addition, you will have the opportunity to pass legislation codifying these decisions with the votes of the new Congress. This Congress will gather on January 9th and retain a solid bipartisan, pro-Ukraine and pro-Israel majority.

And then, I assure you, Joseph Robinette Biden, Jr., your future Wikipedia page will be 90% devoted to the last two months of your lengthy political career.

Black Friday for Ukraine and the World

First published on November 11th, 2024

On the morning of November 9th, only seventy-two hours after Trump's victory in the presidential election, we heard our first idiotic and scurrilous statement emanating from the winner's camp. An advisor and campaign staffer by the name of Bryan Lanza lashed out at Ukraine, claiming it wants to make American soldiers die for the Crimea.

Ukrainian soldiers have been fighting for almost three years now (and incurring huge losses) for both their country and their freedom. But they are also doing it so that Americans do not have to see combat and possibly die in Europe or the Far East. The Ukrainians do not need American troops to defend the hedonistic, developed West from an invasion at the hands of the Russo-Korean horde in the East. But they do need American weapons, which the previous administration has doled out sparingly, with excruciating delays, and with absurd restrictions on how they can be used.

The advisor's remarks were so outrageous that they immediately caused a firestorm on social media. Trump's press secretary had to issue a statement disavowing the remarks, characterizing them as Lanza's personal opinion. That was perhaps the last bit of relatively good news to come out of Washington on November 9th. The worst was yet to come, and it came in the form of the following statement:

"I will not be inviting former Ambassador Nikki Haley, or former Secretary of State Mike Pompeo, to join the Trump Administration, which is currently in formation," Trump stated. "I appreciated working with them previously, and would like to thank them for their service to our country."

This came after several sources familiar with the process reported that Pompeo was being seriously discussed as a possible contender for Secretary of Defense.

Mike Pompeo is an ardent Atlanticist. He was the architect of the highly successful Middle East Policy in the first Trump administration. He supports

Ukraine and had been widely expected to play the same role of wise guardian within a second Trump administration. His plan on Ukraine leaked in July and can be summed up as follows: both sides agree to a cease-fire along the entire existing line of contact. NATO takes on the responsibility of defending (in case of a new Putin attack) every inch of Ukrainian territory on its side of the cease-fire line. The West, meanwhile, will never recognize the territory currently held by Moscow as legally belonging to Russia.

This is not a path for Ukraine to win the war. But it is nevertheless a solid plan under the current circumstances. In essence, we are talking about accepting a divided country into NATO (as we did with West Germany in 1955). For a period of time, Ukraine would lose 20% of its territory. But it would throw off Muscovy's yoke once and for all and be able to integrate itself within the West's security sphere. I believe a majority of Ukrainians would approve this step in a referendum, albeit with a heavy heart.

But now there will be no referendum based on Pompeo's plan. Putin will of course never support such a course of action. As much as Putin seems to be savoring the chunks of Ukrainian territory Russia has seized in the war, they will never be enough for him. He needs all of Ukraine. He craves seeing the West embarrassed, ashamed, and helpless after the former Free World is forced to surrender Ukraine.

At the Valdai Forum on November 7th, Putin positively glowed. He complimented Trump so many times that I am now certain that he already knew that Trump had no plans to include his former foreign policy guru in the new administration. Instead, the president-elect has chosen a path forward offered by a consummate Ukrainophobe, a man Trump appointed as US senator in 2022 and as his running mate in 2024—J. D. Vance. Vance was assigned the task of promoting the plan once it was developed over the course of several sessions of a working group consisting of like-minded individuals (Putin, Trump, and their go-betweens, Carlson, Musk, and Orban). The peace plan that these remarkable men came up with is a plan to destroy the Ukrainian state, a plan to resolve the Ukraine issue once and for all. As with the Pompeo plan, it stipulates a freezing of the conflict. But, whereas the Pompeo plan calls for Ukraine to receive security guarantees from the West according to Article 5 of the NATO charter, the Vance plan forces Ukraine to provide Russia with guarantees of its helplessness. The country would be legally bound to refuse any military aid from the West, including weapon shipments.

The Russians are so generous of heart (as Dostoevsky would say) that they could not possibly remain indifferent to the selection process for Trump's cabinet. I managed to find a remarkable little article from RIA Novosti within the vast expanse of the Russian internet entitled "Americans do not want to see Pompeo on the Trump team." The article cites some anonymous poll alleging that 84% of respondents are against including Pompeo in the new administration.

In any case, events move on. Trump has chosen his "peace plan" for Ukraine. Ukraine will never agree to it. Trump will threaten to stop all weapon shipments. This is what we will see in January and February 2025 most likely. We needed to think about that before. Instead we need to do it now. Starting with taking stock of our assets and analyzing the potential of what remains of the Free World's institutions. A Free World whose guilty smile is vanishing before our eyes like the Cheshire cat's.

The United States

Trump will not appoint Haley or Pompeo to positions within the administration, but he cannot remove recently elected Republicans in both chambers of Congress who on the whole share Haley and Pompeo's pro-Ukraine views rather than Trump and Vance's pro-Russia sentiments. Mike Rogers, Michael McCaul, and Mike Turner, the high-profile leaders of this majority, are the authors of a superb report on Ukraine.[8]

These men worked hard for years to expose the Biden administration's unwillingness to provide sufficient military aid to Ukraine. They managed to overcome strong opposition from Trumpers in Congress and passed a bill to finance this aid. The main objector to the bill? A young senator and absolute lowlife by the name of J. D. Vance.

And now all of Ukraine would love to hear these three respected friends of the nation voice their opinion on Vice-President-elect Vance's peace plan. I hope that we will hear it soon.

---

8   See https://foreignaffairs.house.gov/proposed-plan-for-victory-in-ukraine.

Europe

For decades, Europe has nurtured plans for the establishment of a European army, one capable of defending its borders regardless of what is happening domestically with its transatlantic ally. And then, almost out of nowhere, like Venus emerging from the sea, such an army appeared on the scene. It is called the Ukrainian Armed Forces, and it has been protecting Europe for almost three years now from an invasion at the hands of the horde from the East. But then a complete moron entered the White House and for some reason decided to make this efficient European army surrender. He advised Europe not to rely on this force and to deal with the defense of its borders on its own. To defend against the very barbarians which the Ukrainian Armed Forces had ground down for three years. The existential threat now looming will quickly clear their heads and the fundamental question becomes: can Europe provide weapons shipments to embattled Ukraine when the aforementioned gentleman has stopped them as punishment for the country's refusal to capitulate? The response is a contradictory one—yes and no. It depends on how combat operations unfold. In a stalemate scenario resulting in a protracted war of attrition along the 1000-km line of contact between the sides, the answer is no. Europe simply does not have the production capabilities for ammunition that the US has. By the time Europe develops such capabilities, Ukrainians might no longer exist.

But Europe is surely able to provide Ukraine with the high-tech weaponry needed for a blitz victory. An extraordinary threat calls for the adoption of extraordinary military measures—*hundreds* (!!) of state-of-the-art aircraft (F-16s, Mirages, Typhoons, Gripens) operated by Western volunteer pilots stationed on air bases in Finland, Poland, and Romania. Dozens of Advanced Surface-to-Air Missile Systems (NASAMS) would be absolute game-changers in the Russo-Ukrainian war. They would: 1) establish a de-facto no-fly zone over the entirety of Ukrainian territory, 2) be able to strike Russian aviation deep within Russian territory, and 3) either destroy the Russian alignment of forces in the Crimea or force them to evacuate.

A Ukrainian flag flying over Sevastopol and the symbolic destruction of the Crimean bridge would produce the very current developments on the ground that the dictator in the Kremlin loves to crow about after Russia seizes some Ukrainian village.

I believe that there are about ten countries which together possess such potential and are willing to take such a decisive step to guarantee their security. They will join forces organically with an already existing, battle-hardened European Army. It's not Ukraine that should have to beg to be accepted into some prestigious club. For the nations of Western Civilization there exists only one club worth joining—those countries willing to put a stop to barbarians threatening to destroy this Great Civilization.

Does Trump Want to Be Remembered as Chamberlain or Churchill?

December 1, 2024

My previous, rather gloomy, column [Black Friday for Ukraine and the World] nevertheless included an optimistic note.

> Although Trump will not appoint Pompeo or Haley to positions within his administration, he cannot remove recently elected Republicans in both chambers of Congress who on the whole share Pompeo and Haley's pro-Ukraine views rather than Trump and Vance's pro-Russia sentiments. Michael McCaul, Mike Rogers, and Mike Turner, the high-profile leaders of this majority, are the authors of the superb "Proposed plan for victory in Ukraine."[9] And now it would seem all of Ukraine would like to hear these three distinguished friends of our nation voice their opinion on current totalitarian challenges to the Free World. I hope we will hear them soon...

We did hear their powerful voice six days later. On November 21st, Michael McCaul addressed the Atlantic Council with a speech entitled "Russia and the Authoritarian Challenge." He painted a bleak but very frank picture of a global war that is, for all intents and purposes, already underway:

> Russia was our enemy, an adversary. They still are today. You call it an axis. I call it an unholy alliance that Chairman Xi and

---

9   See https://foreignaffairs.house.gov/proposed-plan-for-victory-in-ukraine/.

Putin made at the Beijing Olympics, two weeks before the invasion of Ukraine. You can't separate the Ayatollah from Putin. Putin invited Hamas to the Kremlin right after October 7th. The alliance between Xi and Putin is clear. North Korea has now sent ten thousand troops into the conflict. We don't choose our enemies. All four of these dictators chose us.

Over the course of the almost three years that this large-scale military conflict has played out, McCaul and his friends have consistently and sharply criticized the Biden administration's response to Putin's aggression, calling it belated, insufficient, and indecisive.

We're projecting weakness, not strength. That would invite more aggression from Putin. It also impacts Chairman Xi and his calculus, looking at Taiwan and the Indo-Pacific. Moldova would certainly fall within a day, as would Georgia. And then, all of Eastern Europe would be under the threat and the dark cloud of Russian domination. We can't afford to lose this fight. Ukrainians are fighting for our national interests and we are betraying them.

But McCaul does not limit himself to criticizing the Biden administration. Without mentioning Trump by name, McCaul is ruthless in addressing the ultra-Trumpist wing of his own party: "I find it very strange. I can't explain it. I suppose there's an isolationist wing within my party that possibly existed in the 1930s." Ambassador John Herbst, the moderator of the Atlantic Council Frontpage event, asked "Why this weird synergy between the weak—one clear weakness in the Biden administration and people who want to make America strong again?" "I don't know. I always ask the question, what would Reagan do? To my Republican colleagues, what would Ronald Reagan do, the guy who brought down the Soviet Union? And now we have these pro-Putin, Russian-loving people. I don't understand it," continued the speaker.

McCaul used this policy speech to stake out a clear position as leader of the bipartisan pro-Ukraine majority in Congress. "You'll have fringes on the left and the right that will never vote for Ukraine but it's the members in the middle, the sensible center, that will bring this coalition together."

McCaul's clearly defined position makes him one of the most important political figures in Washington at this critical juncture in world history. He is fully aware of both the responsibilities and the opportunities that accompany his unique mission. The Congressional Pro-Ukrainian majority has already de-facto blocked the nomination of several of the most odious of Trump's candidates.

From the lectern at the Atlantic Council, that ideological bastion of the Deep State and the Free World, he posed an existential question to us all, but to one person above all else—Donald J. Trump—"Do you want to be remembered as Chamberlain or Churchill?"

The Little Boy from Aleppo and the Little Girl from Vinnitsa

First published on December 9th, 2024

The whole world remembers the three-year-old Syrian boy from Aleppo. He was one of the thousands on whom we successfully tested the latest in Russian weapon systems. While we were busy boasting about its success, this little boy lay dying, promising to make a full report to Allah about what had transpired. At the time I managed to put a few words to paper:

> A child threatening to expose his tormentors by appealing to God is a trope taken right out of Dostoevsky. It is a vital component to his work and to his belief system. I have been an agnostic my entire conscious life, but at that moment I found myself wanting God to exist more fervently than ever before. And hoping that the boy from Aleppo would tell him everything. Tell him about all the "testing," about Putin, Lavrov, Shoigu, Gundyayev. About all of us. We do not deserve sympathy or forgiveness. May we all be damned to hell . . .

It seems the boy from Aleppo was able to make his appeal to Allah after all, and we Russians are in store for a long period of retribution thanks to the incalculable number of crimes against humanity our compatriots committed across the world in our name.

We must also speak of a four-year-old little girl from Vinnitsa named Liza who left us under somewhat different circumstances, free from pain and suffering, at one of those happy moments in her short life. Liza had Down Syndrome, you see, and was on her way to her speech therapist with her mother on a beautiful sunny day, in the best of moods. She was pushing her stroller in front of her, proud as can be of her ability.

"She was so intelligent and capable. Liza loved coming to see us. She was always so excited. A very kind little girl," recalled the therapist.

***

The Almighty (Providence, Mahatma, Universal AI) has already issued his verdict.

They are coming back. Hundreds of thousands of butchers, the ones who survived, are coming back, and this time they will be armed. They signed up to commit murder for money and then became warped by a drug known as impunity, or even glorification, of their run-of-the-mill criminal acts. They are returning to their ancestral home as I write this. Maybe there are only a few of them at the moment. But they might very well flood the gates en masse tomorrow if this "freezing of the conflict" we keep hearing about is instated. People call them "Ukrainians," the same way they called returning soldiers "Afghans" in the 90s. These "Afghans" blew each other up at funerals by the dozens over quotas on the vodka trade. The "Ukrainians," meanwhile, will simply devour the country from within. Nothing will remain.

The Courage of the White Flag

First published on January 4th, 2025

It seems the Argentinian leftist and proponent of liberation theology, the one who rose through the ranks to become God's emissary on Earth, has decided to issue a statement on Ukraine, one candid as it is naive. The Pope articulated what many in the global community were hesitant to discuss in public.

Two opposing wings of the American political spectrum don't really want peace in Ukraine. What they want is for **Ukraine to capitulate**. The left-wing progressives and right-wing isolationists are united in their animosity toward deep-state NATO-centric policy within the US government.

The leaders of Central Europe, unworthy inheritors of the Hungarian (1956) and Czechoslovak (1968) revolutions don't really want peace. They want **Ukraine to capitulate**.

An ever-growing number of "very good" Russians—Schlosberg, Yashin, Yavlinsky, Latynina, Shulman, Pastukhov—don't really want peace. They want **Ukraine to capitulate**. Some of them seem to be preening for an imagined electorate in some future election that will never take place. Others are simply in a rush to put every one of their deeply imperialistic anti-Ukraine complexes on display.

Let's take a closer look at the primary arguments from this "peace" mafia, starting with the foundational one:

Ukraine will never return to its 1991 borders or even to the borders that existed on February 24, 2022.

This is true if the US and the West as a whole continue their three-year policy of "judicious" allocation of military aid (in small increments) to a suffering Ukraine, a nation that, all on its own, has been using the bodies of its soldiers to protect the entire fucking Western world from Rashist aggression.

But this would happen if we saw a significant increase in allied support, something that is economically feasible and would require a minimum amount of political will. This support would entail, first and foremost,

Ukraine receiving a few hundred state-of-the-art aircraft operated by contractor pilots and crews from the West. This is exactly how President Macron of France has outlined a path to Victory for Ukraine when speaking to his counterparts in the alliance.

If we return to the here and now, we can see that a certain in-crowd of global thinkers has convinced itself, after endless repetition of the line that victory for Ukraine (the restoring of its territorial integrity) is no longer possible, that we must put an end to this mindless slaughter and "freeze" the conflict. As a model to follow, they bring up the "freezing" of the Korean conflict, agreed to in July of 1953 and in effect to this very day.

The task of implementing this "freezing" of the Ukraine conflict will be taken up by a team within the administration of President-elect Donald Trump. But unlike his predecessor Dwight Eisenhower, who achieved a "freezing" of the war in Korea, thereby securing prosperous growth for South Korea for 70 years, Trump is making two grave (I would even add, treasonous) mistakes.

First of all, Trump does not view the conflict as World War IV, a conflict started by totalitarian regimes against the Free World. Instead, he sees himself as some sort of neutral mediator, ready to punish both sides depending on their willingness to negotiate.

And General Eisenhower would certainly not have deigned to discuss security guarantees for South Korea with communist gangsters such as Kim, Mao, or Stalin. He discussed them with South Korea and South Korea only. He signed a joint defense treaty and left behind a 100-thousand strong expeditionary force on its territory.

Trump's team, on the other hand, is starting out with public assurances to Putin that Ukraine will never receive this or that security guarantee (according to the plan Vance has articulated). This is all music to Putin's ears, of course, and provides him the opportunity to achieve his one maniacal objective: the destruction of the Ukrainian state, something he was unable to achieve militarily.

Putin intends to draw up a plan with Trump's approval that both "freezes" the war in Ukraine and renders the country defenseless (most likely this has already happened using Carlson and Orban as intermediaries). Trump will then attempt to foist this agreement onto Ukraine by threatening to cease arm shipments. A serious political crisis will begin to develop in the country. The war has worn down the Ukrainian people; most are in a state of deep fatigue and are wary of losing the West's support. People might begin looking around for a Ukrainian Petain/Kadar/Husak/Jaruzelski. After all, the talking points for such a figure can be found in many of Arestovich's statements.

It bears mentioning that every one of the historical figures listed above was only a posteriori viewed as a traitor. They rose to prominence at first as fully competent leaders, sincere in their desire to save the Fatherland. In order to preserve their nation, however, they suggested collaborating with a Fascist aggressor.

The last thing I want to do from far-away Washington, DC is to call on Ukraine to fight to the very last Ukrainian. I am fully aware of how utterly exhausted Ukrainian society is. What I will do, however, is call on all these budding Petains and Kadars to give it a rest with their ideas and initiatives. Things may change drastically on the strategic level in the very near future.

What if Trump comes to the realization rather soon, let's say the beginning of February, that he is unable to get Putin and Zelensky to agree on the "freezing" of the conflict. Zelensky is for the freezing of the war but also seeks actual physical security guarantees for the rest of Ukraine. Putin is for a freezing of the war that leaves Ukraine completely defenseless.

Since Trump has promoted his plan for Ukraine so often and with such zeal, he will be forced to find a scapegoat when discussions go south. He will then mete out a punishment. The President-elect has never been known for his fondness for Ukraine. Those closest to him (Vance, Musk, Carlson, Trump, Jr.) are outright Ukrainophobes.

But Trump also has only the slimmest of majorities in both chambers of Congress; he cannot simply ignore the Reaganesque, pro-Ukraine wing of the Republican party (McCaul, Rogers, Turner, Haley, Pompeo), especially when their position is so well-articulated:

"We cannot afford to lose this fight. Ukrainians are fighting for our national interests and we are betraying them."

In a month or so we will know the results of ongoing discussions on this topic within the Republican party. European heads of state are not keen to sit back and wait out these talks, however. If Washington decides to betray Ukraine, it's these European countries that will be threatened with extinction. And, yes, the West is fully capable of betraying those who put their trust in it and its ideals. There are tons of examples. But Europeans have been yearning for a European Army for decades; they won't commit collective suicide at such a critical moment in their history by refusing to provide tangible combat support when just such an army miraculously appears and proceeds to defend them from the Rashist Horde for three years now, all on its own.

Or does one have to be Asiatic, like Erdogan or Aliyev, to properly stand up to a rat that has crawled out of the sewers of St. Petersburg?

How the "Grown-ups" in the White House Can Win World War IV

First published on February 9th, 2025

To begin with, they can't act like Tillerson. They need to model themselves after Pompeo. As we all know, Tillerson lasted just over a year as Secretary of State. Then, when he couldn't take it anymore, he called Trump a moron in a moment of pique. With that, he slammed the door and handed in his resignation.

In came Pompeo to replace him, impressing upon State Department officials that "Trump is not a moron. He is simply an unconventional genius." Trump, ever the professional showman, played the role of unconventional genius to the hilt in the Middle East with Pompeo in the director's chair. In fact, he played it so well that world leaders began to think that he was the one behind the Abraham Accords.

The grown-ups in the White House must appeal to the unconventional genius's personal interests when persuading him to take action in the foreign policy realm. They must remember he thinks of himself as the leader of the entire world, someone with no rivals. Let no amount of flattery go to waste, even in its crudest forms. If they aren't willing to lick Trump's ass, their most bitter geopolitical enemies will polish it until it shines, starting with his ex-KGB handler in the Kremlin. He is already chomping at the bit to get his chance to do some polishing. It's something straight out of Yesenin and his Khlopusha: "Lead me to his presence, lead me to him, I want to see this man!"[10]

---

10 A reference to a quote from Khlopusha.

Putin wants to "see this man" so that he can smooth-talk him in two hours flat into being his obedient lapdog, just like he did in Helsinki.

Trump and Putin shake hands during the G20 summit in Osaka on June 28, 2019.[11]

He considers himself, with some justification, to be the alpha male in this relationship. Under no circumstances must the grown-ups allow this unconventional genius to remain alone in a room with such a professional manipulator.

In order to work effectively with their client, the grown-ups need to come up with an explanation that fits Trump's unconventional mind to frame the war currently waging across the globe. His clip-thinking consciousness has been ruptured; it is incapable of seeing connections between what is happening in the Middle East, Ukraine, and the Pacific Rim. It is a given that Trump must be at the center of any proposed plan; he must be the global demiurge and future Victor in the Final World War:

Totalitarian regimes the world over, filled with centuries of hatred towards the West, were watching intently as the reputational catastrophe

---

11 This photo is licensed under the Creative Commons Attribution 4.0 International license; the source is http://www.kremlin.ru/events/president/news/60842/photos.

that was the US's withdrawal from Afghanistan unfolded live on television screens across the globe. These regimes took this failed withdrawal as a sign of fundamental weakness within the decadent and hedonistic (as they saw it) Western civilization and looked on with satisfaction as its establishment began to surrender its global leadership role. The three horsemen of this geopolitical underworld—China, Russia, and Iran—now free to act with impunity (the US is gone and they can get away with anything), threw down the gauntlet to the Free World by announcing their intentions to destroy, in a deliberate manner, three sovereign nations—Taiwan, Ukraine, and Israel.

The initial reaction from the United States—the leader of the Free World—was shameful and did nothing but encourage its enemies. The head of the CIA—that traitor Burns—traveled to Moscow and offered Putin a behind-the-scenes promise. He wouldn't allow Ukraine, the only victim of aggression here, to conduct retaliatory strikes on Russian territory. The agency under his leadership then released its professional prediction for an invasion: Kyiv would fall in a week, two at most.

But Burns was wrong. The first climactic battle of World War IV took place at Hostomel and resulted in a miracle on the Dnieper—the horde was soundly defeated. Those 300 symbolic Ukrainian Spartans saved Western civilization from a barbarian invasion and literally dragged the United States by the scruff of the neck back onto the world stage.

About a year and a half later, with the West still in the throes of a cowardly indecisiveness, Iran embarked on its multipronged operation to destroy Israel. And with that a fourth horseman appeared in that Shining City on a Hill.

A new political reality had begun to take shape in Washington. The far-left (progressive) wing of the Democratic Party and its accompanying ideology became almost fanatically invested in a World War IV unleashed by totalitarian regimes. The progressives sided 100% with the tyrants and the bandits. After all, they had loathed the "Imperial West" since their college years and wanted to see it defeated. Their professors at Harvard and Yale, you see, had drummed it into them that this west was guilty of centuries of crimes against the world's oppressed nations.

At the moment there are not that many progressives in Congress, but they do wield great influence at "quality" media outlets. As far as World War IV is concerned, these outlets essentially serve as propaganda mouthpieces for Hamas on the Israeli front and for Putin on the Ukrainian one.

These progressives demand an immediate cease-fire both in the Middle East and in Ukraine—in other words a kind of Afghanistan on steroids—with another embarrassing US withdrawal from the world stage.

Trump's victory in the presidential elections was first and foremost a triumph over these progressives—the fourth horseman of the geopolitical apocalypse. His election has essentially untied the West's hands at a critical moment and given it a unique window of opportunity to achieve a larger, historic victory over all its enemies. What's more, this victory will be more of a conceptual, theoretical one and will not result in a significant loss of human life.

Iran is an easy fix. No boots on the ground will be required from the West. Israel will simply conduct one devastating strike (perhaps with US participation for certain specialized facilities). After that, the rebuilding of what used to be Iran will fall to the country's resurgent urban youth along with a joint Turkish-Azerbaijani military force, deployed in the Iranian part of Azerbaijan to protect its countrymen.

The cowardly, over-cautious (or consciously traitorous) Biden administration never permitted Ukraine to exploit its spectacular successes at the outset of the war and achieve Victory in 2022 or 2023 (a return to 1991 borders and complete restoration of the country's territorial integrity). Instead, the conflict changed shape and became an exhausting war of attrition, a circumstance not at all in Ukraine's favor.

People then began discussing in earnest a "Korea scenario" for freezing the conflict. Cognizant of the Russian people's historic contribution to an Allied victory in WWII and keen to prevent the loss of hundreds of thousands more Russian and Ukrainian lives, President Trump made a unique offer to the dictator in the Kremlin—he would pull Putin out of the gruesome mess he got himself into as a vassal to China.

For this, he must agree to cease all combat activity along the line of contact. Of course, there will be no recognition of his territorial gains. He will be allowed to keep them for a certain amount of time and remain in power in Russia, after he tells his obsequious minions that victory has been achieved, of course.

Western troops will guarantee that the main part of Ukraine remains safe and prosperous (as was the case with Korea). It doesn't really matter what they are called—peacekeepers, volunteers, contractors . . .

The majority of these troops will come from Europe. Trump has called on Europe for years to take on more responsibility for its own security. The very real threat hanging over the continent at the moment only serves to strengthen Trump's argument. Macron has long been trying to persuade his counterparts that EU countries must play a role in Ukraine.

Europe has wished for its own army for decades. But, as Zelensky correctly noted in Davos, "For the first time in 75 years, Europe has its own army, one capable of stopping the Eastern horde. It is the Armed Forces of Ukraine plus aircraft provided by Europe."

This new resolve we are seeing from Europe will allow the West to effectively provide for Ukraine's security in the same way that President Eisenhower in his day provided for the security of South Korea—by deploying an expeditionary Allied force.

If Putin chooses to decline Trump's offer, he loses everything. It is no coincidence that the Putin propaganda machine has been sending out trial balloons of late that seek to justify accepting the offer: "We have already won! We have seized a land corridor to the Crimea and weakened the Ukrainian army!"

It's a fitting resolution really—the Putin regime is destroyed while Putin temporarily keeps his head and his throne along with his famous suitcase toilet.

President Trump believes, with good reason, that communist China is the US's most powerful and dangerous enemy. But until recently this indisputable fact has led him to come to the totally incorrect conclusion. He thought the key to countering the Chinese threat was to settle two conflicts he saw as nothing but distractions—those in Ukraine and in the Middle East. It was a colossal mistake.

It is precisely these wars—waged by two great peoples, Ukrainian and Israeli, at enormous cost and suffering—that have provided the Free World with a unique opportunity to remove the China threat once and for all. And without shedding a drop of blood.

I strongly believe that a double beheading (Iran and Russia), for all the world to see, would force the remaining head of this Chinese dragon to come to its senses and forget about its hostile intentions vis-a-vis an independent Taiwan and any plans for a political and military confrontation with the US. Comrade Xi and his remaining head will be forced to embark on a pilgrimage to the Canossa of our day—Washington DC. I suspect, however, that it will be a different Chinese comrade making the trip.

There is one major obstacle preventing the client from making full use of the pedagogic material set forth above—his manic obsession with winning a Nobel Peace Prize. This fixation gives Putin a massive amount of recruiting potential. He will thank Trump for his offer, gaze at him with devoted, admiring eyes, and promise to provide any support needed in his quest for the Nobel. His territorial demands will be strikingly modest. But what he will do is smooth-talk Trump into including a couple of innocent lines into the final peace agreement about "security guarantees for Russia." And then, after Trump receives his deserved Nobel, Putin will use these "guarantees" to come for the rest of Ukraine.

Trump's obsession with a Nobel Peace Prize (he is absurdly jealous of Obama) might just disappear when he will be presented with a much more impressive red carpet into the history books.

President Woodrow Wilson won World War I.

President Franklin D. Roosevelt won World War II.

President Ronald Reagan won World War III (the Cold War).

All three of these great American presidents were certain that they had won the final World War. Unfortunately, each victory contained a flaw that inevitably led to the next global conflict.

President Donald Trump has been presented with a mission of epic proportions—to defeat the Empire of Evil in the Fourth and Final World War, to do it with relatively little effort and resources spent, and all within the first 100 days of his second presidential term.

End of the Beginning

The events of June 13th on the Middle Eastern front of World War IV have the potential, in my opinion, to profoundly impact the outcome of this war. Israeli forces carried out a brazen operation, unprecedented in the history of global military strategy. They achieved absolute air dominance over a country that is 75 times larger than Israel and has 10 times the population.

The aging ayatollahs—the spiritual leaders of this enormous nation—have indoctrinated their subjects for decades (not trying to hide it from the world at large) that the sacred purpose of Iran's very existence is the destruction of the state of Israel and the extermination of the Jewish people. In pursuit of this "religious" goal, they ramped up their nuclear missile program and surrounded Israel with a band of terrorist proxy regimes.

The horrific and barbaric terrorist attack on Israel of October 7th, 2023, inspired, funded, and organized by Iran, showed the world that the religious thinkers in the country had moved to the implementation stage of their long-planned Second Holocaust.

I am certain that the ayatollahs' resolve was in many respects strengthened by the tepid, underwhelming reaction in the West to Putin's long-standing aggreZZion towards Ukraine.

The Biden administration was technically an ally but its cowardly restrictions on the use of Western weaponry forced Ukraine to wage war with one hand tied behind its back. With Trump and his MAGA-ideology of extreme isolationism in the White House, things did not look good for Israel and perhaps even worse for Ukraine (which Trump is not overly fond of, to put it mildly).

This alarming and uncertain state of affairs led Israel to launch the brilliant operation it dubbed "Rising Lion." Its goal? The seamless destruction of Iran's nuclear weapon arsenal and the removal of an existential threat to the Jewish people.

The operation's success provoked heated discussions in Washington, especially among those closest to Trump. The most prominent MAGA-ites

(Bannon, Carlson, Vance) condemned Israel and spoke out forcefully against the US providing any military support for the operation.

On the other side, we had more traditional Reagan Republicans close to Trump (Cruz, Graham) urging the president at a minimum to deploy American fighter jets to destroy Iran's underground facility at Fordow. For a week or so we saw Trump give incoherent, contradictory statements and then, on Friday evening, he finally gave the order. He had made the decision, however, a few days earlier, when he exclaimed with pride: "*We* have complete control over Iranian airspace!"

The MAGA fanatics were beside themselves at their leader's "betrayal." But Trump has never actually been a fan of MAGA. What he has been and always will be is a MEGAlomaniac. He used his MAGA supporters as a pool of votes and in his first 100 days in office toyed with the idea of somehow translating its ideology into a Nobel Peace Prize. But Netanyahu stepped in and proposed something even more mind-blowing in its grandeur—the glory to be had as the Great American President who proved Victorious in our current World War IV.

Both Netanyahu and Putin recruited the uneducated dimwit in the White House with the same straightforward method—they flattered Trump endlessly and made him feel comfortable on a physiological level. So comfortable, in fact, that their client genuinely looked forward to the next session.* But they were trying to achieve different goals: Putin needed Trump "the peacemaker" who would push Ukraine to capitulate, while Netanyahu needed Trump the military ally who would receive all the laurels befitting a Vanquisher. Netanyahu was very close to his cherished goal on June 21st when he forced Trump to put a decisive end to Iran's nuclear program. The president launched bunker-busting bombs at Fardow, a key nuclear facility unreachable by Israeli aircraft. But then Netanyahu got complacent. The ayatollahs should have been executed the very next day, starting with the Supreme Leader, for the heinous crimes they committed against the citizens of Israel. If Netanyahu had done this, Trump would have been unable to backtrack; he would have been permanently drawn into the World War IV Great Victor scenario.

But Netanyahu underestimated just how much pressure the MAGA zealots were putting on Trump at that time. Of course, Trump's *fucking* ceasefire took away from the brilliance of the military operation but in the

---

* Mark Rutte, the NATO Secretary General, outdid them both at the June 25th summit, providing a master class in how to deal with a megalomaniac.

grand scheme of things, nothing really changed. Israel still has complete air dominance over Iranian territory and at any moment can take out every last ayatollah along with the more odious generals within the IRGC. What's more, I presume last week President Aliyev of Azerbaijan pre-recorded a future address to the nation:

"Brothers and Sisters, I am here to make an address to you, my friends. The fall of the criminal regime in Tehran has given rise to an atmosphere of lawlessness and chaos in the majority of Iranian territory. In light of this, my primary concern as the head of state of Azerbaijan must be the safety of 25 million of our countrymen. I just spoke with my friend and brother President Erdogan . . ."

An unqualified Israeli victory over Iran, so well-deserved for the IDF, that is then botched (postponed?) by Trump would have an enormous political and psychological impact on the Rashist political establishment. This is not conjecture. This is an empirical fact. The cries of utter despair we heard in the propaganda cesspools of the Kremlin on June 23rd, when it seemed Russia's "strategic partner" had been taken out, turned to gleeful sighs of relief the next morning when they learned the worst had not come to pass.

As for the current situation on the Ukrainian front, it's probably a good thing that the Coalition of the Willing (Ukraine, Germany, France, the UK) will not have to deal with the "peacemaker" in Washington constantly underfoot.

Under close supervision by the Reagan Republicans in Congress, Trump will sell the Europeans the weapons Ukraine needs. The most important lesson of the last few days for the Coalition of the Willing is not to repeat the mistake Netanyahu made. As soon as Trump makes the slightest overture towards *fucking* peacemaking, they need to take a page from the Ukrainian sailor when he addressed that RuZZian warship.

Concerning the outcome of World War IV, what I have outlined above brings to mind Winston Churchill's remark of cautious optimism from November 10th, 1942, after the Allied victory at El-Alamein: "Now this is not the end. It is not even the beginning of the end. But it is, perhaps, the end of the beginning."